Microsoft Exchange Server 2016 Administration Guide

Deploy, Manage and Administer Microsoft Exchange Server 2016

Edward van Biljon

Distributors:

BPB PUBLICATIONS
20, Ansari Road, Darya Ganj
New Delhi-110002
Ph: 23254990/23254991

DECCAN AGENCIES
4-3-329, Bank Street,
Hyderabad-500195
Ph: 24756967/24756400

MICRO MEDIA
Shop No. 5, Mahendra Chambers,
150 DN Rd. Next to Capital Cinema,
V.T. (C.S.T.) Station, MUMBAI-400 001
Ph: 22078296/22078297

BPB BOOK CENTRE
376 Old Lajpat Rai Market,
Delhi-110006
Ph: 23861747

Published by Manish Jain for BPB Publications, 20 Ansari Road, Darya Ganj, New Delhi-110002 and Printed at Repro India Ltd, Mumbai

Dedicated to

Everyone taking the time to learn
My passion has always been teaching and upskilling
others so that one day they can do the same.

About the Author

Edward van Biljon is an experienced Exchange specialist, who for the past 17 years, has been working with customers on all levels of Exchange and helping them design solutions for their environments and also migrating Exchange on-premise to the cloud.

He has also worked for Microsoft in the PFE space and big corporates and has been awarded the Office Apps and Services MVP award for the past four years.

Edward has been writing articles/blogs on his blog but also for Experts Exchange, TechGenix, and other companies.

Outside of work, Edward spends a lot of his time on the Technet Forums, 3rd party forums, and blogs answering questions and writing articles to assist others in the Technical space.

Acknowledgement

I want to thank a few people for their support throughout my career. I want to thank my wife for standing by me all the years I have been studying to get to where I am today and for always pushing me to be my best! To my family and friends, thank you for all your love and support and for constantly checking in to see how I am doing and motivating me to continue.

To JJ Milner, who is a true leader and who motivates, pushes you to do your best all the time. I would also like to mention Bernard Kur, and if he were a General, I would love to serve under his team. Thank you for always being there as a friend but also as a mentor, your love and passion for people are just amazing.

Thank you to BPB for allowing me to write this book, and thank you for your support.

Preface

Exchange 2016, one of the flagship Exchange versions out there has changed the game for how you not only manage your server but also how email systems and delivery has improved.

From slimming down the roles to just 2 in Exchange 2016, Exchange 2016 now only consists of a Mailbox role, and everything else is now a service, like your Hub Transport, Client Access Service, unified messaging. Lastly, the Edge role, still available in this version, can be used in your DMZ.

Exchange 2016 has also evolved and gone back versions you could virtualize your servers, but the way underlying hypervisors handle these servers shows you the effort put into a product.

From a security perspective, Microsoft is putting everything into ensuring the security of Exchange 2016. If they find something, then a patch is released to ensure that the specific problem in question is addressed. Many Admins don't feel the need to upgrade as they are on a version that "works"; however, they still introduce risk to the environment.

The installation of Exchange 2016 is not difficult at all. Once all the prerequisites are done, you can do your installation unattended, using the GUI or script it like some MVP's have done. Scripting makes everything easier as everything is covered from start to finish in a single script.

The primary goal of this book is to teach you about Exchange 2016, how to deploy a new server or coexistence with Exchange 2010 or Exchange 2013. This book contains sample scripts, how to create a DAG or a mailbox database, how to perform mailbox moves etc.

Over the next 11 chapters, you will learn the following:

Chapter 1 Introduction to Exchange 2016 and understanding how things work, what has changed from legacy versions to get your server ready for installation.

Chapter 2 discusses how to install Exchange 2016, how to prepare your Virtual machine, network cards, and chatting about IPv4 and IPv6. Finally, we discuss installing Exchange 2016 using the unattended method and the GUI method.

Chapter 3, with Exchange 2016 installed, we now need to configure our server. In this chapter, we learn how to use the EAC and EMS as well as understanding licensing and configuring your connectors.

Chapter 4 is a continuation of Chapter 3 with creating and configuring SSL certificates and how to import and export them as well as configuring your virtual directories. We have some sample PowerShell cmdlets that shows you how to configure them using the EMS.

Chapter 5 is a key chapter as it discusses the client connectivity methods; this includes POP3, IMAP4, ActiveSync, MAPI, Outlook Anywhere, and we also speak about how Mac clients connect.

Chapter 6 is the main chapter as it speaks about how to configure your storage, how you can create your mailbox databases using the EAC and EMS, as well as creating a Database Availability Group, and we speak about failover clustering and also circular logging and backups.

Chapter 7 describes how public folders have changed since Exchange 2010, and the first change happened in Exchange 2013. We also chat about how you can migrate your public folders from legacy to Exchange 2016.

Chapter 8 briefly describes unified messaging in Exchange 2016 and how to perform migrations from legacy versions.

Chapter 9 describes how to perform mailbox migrations using batches and also performing mailbox moves and includes some sample scripts. We also cover corruption and how it affects mailbox moves and, lastly, how you can increase the default MRS values to run more mailbox migrations.

Chapter 10 describes how to configure WinRM and how to use the EAC and EMS as well as viewing the commands run from the EAC.

Chapter 11 describes the common issues that happen in Exchange 2016 and how you can overcome them.

Errata

We take immense pride in our work at BPB Publications and follow best practices to ensure the accuracy of our content to provide with an indulging reading experience to our subscribers. Our readers are our mirrors, and we use their inputs to reflect and improve upon human errors if any, occurred during the publishing processes involved. To let us maintain the quality and help us reach out to any readers who might be having difficulties due to any unforeseen errors, please write to us at :

errata@bpbonline.com

Your support, suggestions and feedbacks are highly appreciated by the BPB Publications' Family.

Table of Contents

CHAPTER 1
Introduction to Exchange 2016

Welcome to Exchange 2016 in-depth. In this chapter, we will be taking a look at getting your environment ready for Exchange 2016 and what the list of requirements are. We also take a look at coexistence scenarios and supported coexistence setups plus ending off the chapter with a brief discussion on IISCrypto and how you can secure your server and also load balancers and taking a look at Cumulative updates.

Structure

The topics to be covered in this chapter are:

- Introduction to Exchange 2016
- Changes in Exchange 2016 vs. 2013 and 2010
- Domain requirements
- PrepareAD and PrepareSchema commands
- Coexistence
- Prerequisites
- .NET framework

- UCMA 4.0 requirement
- IISCrypto – Understanding protocols to be locked down.
- Explaining cumulative updates.

Objectives

- Learn about Exchange 2016 and how it has changed from Legacy versions.
- Understand the prerequisites to run the Exchange 2016 installation.
- Run in a coexistence environment.
- Lockdown your environment.
- Understand how Cumulative Updates work in Exchange 2016.

Introduction to Exchange 2016

Exchange 2016 is an on-premise email server that allows an organization to have its end users to connect Outlook to and to be able to send/receive the email. Exchange 2016 is by no means the first on-premise Exchange server, Exchange goes back a long way to version 5.5.

In time, a lot has improved in the newer versions and with the newer versions they are easily scalable and today can be built quickly to create a highly available on-premise solution. Exchange 2016 RTM was released on 01 October 2015 and has been around for a few years.

Exchange 2016 is the last version that can coexist with Exchange 2010 and is the migration path to the cloud as well if your company has skipped Exchange 2013.

Changes in Exchange 2016 vs. 2013 vs. 2010

With each new version of Exchange, something new is added and other things are removed or become redundant. Here is a table of some of the changes in each version and you will notice the key differences in each:

	Exchange 2016	Exchange 2013	Exchange 2010
Roles	2 (MBX/Edge)	2 (MBX/Edge)	5 (CHUME)
Unified messaging	Y	Y	Y
Outlook clients	See Matrix	See Matrix	See Matrix
Public folders	Mailbox	Mailbox	Database (no redundancy)
Server support	Server 2012/R2/Server 2016	Server 2012/R2/Server 2016	Server 2008 R2/Server 2012/Server 2012 R2

Table 1.1: Difference of roles

- **MBX** – Stands for **Mailbox**
- **CHUME** – Stands for **CAS/HUB/Unified Messaging, Mailbox and Edge**

Exchange Server supportability Matrix: **https://docs.microsoft.com/en-us/exchange/plan-and-deploy/supportability-matrix?view=exchserver-2019**

Domain requirements

With Exchange, you need to ensure that you are running the correct domain controllers and that your forest levels are on the correct level as well for things to work properly. Exchange 2016 supports the following domain controllers:

- Windows Server 2019 standard or datacenter
- Windows Server 2016 standard or datacenter
- Windows Server 2012 R2 standard or datacenter
- Windows Server 2012 standard or datacenter
- Windows 2008 R2 standard or enterprise
- Windows 2008 R2 datacenter RTM or higher

If you have earlier versions of Windows servers that are domain controllers, you will need to upgrade them to newer supported servers. Your Active Directory Forest Functional level also needs to be at a minimum of Windows Server 2008 R2 or higher. To be able to have Exchange running, you need to have a domain controller in your environment, Exchange cannot install without a valid domain controller and that domain controller needs to be a **Global Catalog (GC)** and needs to be writeable.

Running a windows server with just IPv6 is not supported, you need to have IPv4 running in conjunction with IPv6.

PrepareAD and PrepareSchema commands

The 2x commands listed above are normally required to be run prior to an installation or upgrade of Exchange 2016. The Exchange 2016 setup whether run in GUI or unattended mode does the `PrepareAD` at the beginning of the installation if you do not perform the command.

Microsoft recommends that in smaller environments you let the wizard handling upgrading the schema. However in larger environments or if you have different teams handling Exchange and Active Directory then you should run the commands:

"Setup.exe /IAcceptExchangeServerLicenseTerms /PrepareSchema" and "Setup.exe / IAcceptExchangeServerLicenseTerms /PrepareAD"

It is essential that the account running these commands is a member of the following groups:

- Domain Admins
- Schema Admins
- Enterprise Admin
- Organization Management

If you are running multiple domains in a forest, then you need to run the command:

"Setup.exe /IAcceptExchangeServerLicenseTerms / PrepareAllDomains"

Or if you want to prepare a specific domain then instead of using `/PrepareAllDomains`, you would use `/PrepareDomain:mydomain.com` as an example.

The `PrepareAD` command also ensures that all your security groups in the Exchange OU are populated. If you have mistakenly deleted them or the groups are corrupted, it will create new ones once you run this command.

Be sure to read the release notes on the Cumulative Update you are installing if it does have a newer version to upgrade to.

Coexistence

Exchange 2016 can coexist with earlier versions of Exchange to allow you to do migrations. You need to be aware though, to be able to install Exchange 2016 in an environment running Exchange 2010 or 2013, your older servers need to be on a certain Rollup (Exchange 2010) and **cumulative update (CU)** for it to work together.

Exchange 2007 is not supported at all in coexistence with Exchange 2016. If you try and do the installation, it will fail as it detects the legacy versions of Exchange. If you are running Exchange 2010, you need to be on Exchange 2010 SP3 Rollup 11 or higher, this includes your Edge Transport servers.

If you are running Exchange 2013, you need to be on Exchange 2013 Cumulative Update 10 or higher, again this includes your Edge transport Servers.

Server prerequisites

Before you can deploy any version of Exchange, this includes Exchange 2013, 2016 and 2019, there is a list of prerequisites that need to be completed before you attempt to launch the setup of Exchange.

Here is the list of prerequisites needed to prepare Active Directory:

- .NET Framework 4.8 or higher (this is the new requirement as of writing this in January 2020)
- Visual C++ 2013 Redistributable Package.
- Remote Tool Administration Pack.

Below is the list of prerequisites for a Mailbox Server running on Windows Server 2016 (take note of the order of things):

- .NET Framework 4.8 or higher
- KB3206632

- Visual C++ 2012 redistributable
- Visual C++ 2013 redistributable
- Microsoft Unified Communications API 4.0 (UCMA)

To install the Windows Features, you need to run the following PowerShell command and then reboot your server:

- Install-WindowsFeature NET-Framework-45-Features, Server-Media-Foundation, RPC-over-HTTP-proxy, RSAT-Clustering, RSAT-Clustering-CmdInterface, RSAT-Clustering-Mgmt, RSAT-Clustering-PowerShell, WAS-Process-Model, Web-Asp-Net45, Web-Basic-Auth, Web-Client-Auth, Web-Digest-Auth, Web-Dir-Browsing, Web-Dyn-Compression, Web-Http-Errors, Web-Http-Logging, Web-Http-Redirect, Web-Http-Tracing, Web-ISAPI-Ext, Web-ISAPI-Filter, Web-Lgcy-Mgmt-Console, Web-Metabase, Web-Mgmt-Console, Web-Mgmt-Service, Web-Net-Ext45, Web-Request-Monitor, Web-Server, Web-Stat-Compression, Web-Static-Content, Web-Windows-Auth, Web-WMI, Windows-Identity-Foundation, RSAT-ADDS

Below is the list of prerequisites for the Edge Transport Role running on Windows Server 2016. (Take note of the order of things):

- .NET Framework 4.8 or higher
- Visual C++ 2012 redistributable.

The PowerShell command to install the Windows Feature is as follows:

```
Install-WindowsFeature ADLDS
```

To be able to manage your Exchange 2016 Server from another machine, you need to install the Exchange 2016 Management Tools.

> **Take note that it is only supported on Windows 10 and Windows 8.1**

Exchange 2016 tools running on Windows 10

There are also some requirements that have to be met to run the tools, here are the requirements:

- Install Visual C++ 2012 redistributable.

You need to enable the following windows features on your system and you can do so by running this PowerShell command from an elevated PowerShell prompt:

- Enable-WindowsOptionalFeature -Online
  -FeatureName IIS-ManagementScriptingTools,IIS-
  ManagementScriptingTools,IIS-
  IIS6ManagementCompatibility,IIS-LegacySnapIn,IIS-
  ManagementConsole,IIS-Metabase,IIS-
  -WebServerManagementTools,IIS-WebServerRole

Exchange 2016 tools running on Windows 8.1

There is one additional requirement on Windows 8.1, here is the list of items that need to be installed:

- .NET Framework 4.8 or higher
- Visual C++ 2012 Redistributable.

You need to enable the following windows features on your system and you can do so by running this PowerShell command from an elevated PowerShell prompt:

- Enable-WindowsOptionalFeature -Online -FeatureName
  IIS-ManagementScriptingTools,IIS-ManagementScripting
  Tools,IIS-IIS6ManagementCompatibility,IIS-
  LegacySnapIn,IIS-ManagementConsole,IIS-Metabase,IIS-
  WebServerManagementTools,IIS-WebServerRole

Once you have installed the optional windows features, reboot your machine for the changes to take effect.

.NET framework

This is always a big question when it comes to installing .NET Framework on Exchange servers. Microsoft has a matrix that they keep up-to-date on a regular basis and this outlines what version is supported with each version of Exchange.

Here is a small table of what is currently supported on each version of Exchange as of January 2020:

Exchange 2016	Exchange 2013	Exchange 2010
4.7.2 (RTM and CU1 – CU13/14)	4.7.2 (CU21, 22 and 23)	4.5 (SP3)
4.8 (CU13 and above)	4.8 (CU23 and above)	4.8 (Not Supported)

Table 1.2: .NET Framework supported versions

The challenge comes in when updates are released to servers either with **System Center Configuration Manager (SCCM)** or WSUS and installed on the servers. This causes the servers to behave erratically or it breaks things like ActiveSync, etc. Microsoft does provide rollback methods but sometimes you need to recover a server to get it back to a working state.

The next challenge is when you are running Windows Server 2016 and manually check for updates, everything in the list will be installed and again this will cause issues for your version.

Take note of what version is supported for your Exchange environment, Installing the wrong update or version can lead to downtime and missed SLA's.

If a version is not shown in the support matrix, do not attempt to install it as they are not supported by Microsoft. If you are running an earlier **Cumulative Update (CU)** version, check the requirements for that release and update .NET Framework and then immediately upgrade to the higher CU. The Matrix can be viewed in the link below, still valid in January 2020:

https://docs.microsoft.com/en-us/exchange/plan-and-deploy/ supportability-matrix?view=exchserver-2019

UCMA 4.0 requirement

In legacy versions of Exchange (Exchange 2010), you had a role for Unified Communications. With Exchange 2013 this changed to a service and it is the same in Exchange 2016. UCMA stands for *Unified Communications Managed* API that allows you to build applications that provide access to Microsoft Enhanced Presence along with Instant messaging, telephonic and video calls and conferencing.

When you see instant messaging, the first thing that comes to mind is Skype for Business or Lync? In Exchange 2016, you can configure your dial plans and connect to your audio devices like audio codecs, etc. Without this file, the setup will fail as it is a requirement for the mailbox server role. In later versions of Exchange (Exchange 2019), you still need to install UCMA 4.0 even though it has been depreciated in that build.

IISCrypto – Understanding protocols to be locked down

In the world today, if your server is exposed with weak protocols or ciphers it can potentially be attacked by the guys that do ransomware or malware and your server can become an open relay where they hijack your server to send out spam. There are a few settings in Schannel that you can configure to lock down the following:

- Protocols
- Ciphers
- Hashes
- Key Exchanges

Protocols – These are the following:

- TLS
- SSL
- PCT
- Multi-Protocol

Most companies now days only accept TLS 1.2 and Office 365 is phasing out TLS 1.0 and TLS 1.1. I would remove TLS 1.0 and TLS 1.1 and only have your server run TLS 1.2.

Ciphers – These include the following:

- DES
- RC2
- RC4
- Triple DES
- AES 128 and 256

As with the protocols, the ciphers you should look at having enabled are 4 and 5.

Hashes – These include the following:

- MD5
- SHA
- SHA 256
- SHA 384
- SHA 512

With the Hashes, you disable MD5 and leave the rest enabled.

Key Exchanges – These include the following:

- Diffie-Hellman
- PKCS
- ECDH

We disable number 1 as it is a weak Key Exchange these days and leave the last 2 enabled. To modify this easily, you can use a tool called IIS Crypto (version), and each section is listed for you to make the changes. Here is an example of the tool and the options selected as mentioned above:

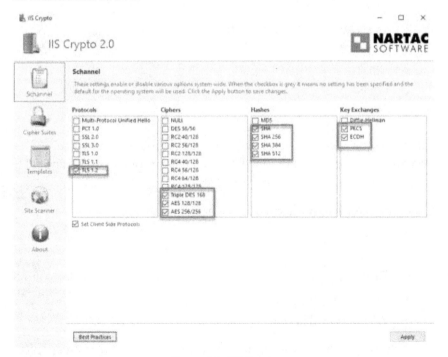

Figure 9.1: IIS Crypto

Once you have made the changes above, click the **apply** button and you will be required to reboot your server.

Explaining Cumulative Updates

Microsoft releases Cumulative Updates, also referred to at CU's every 3 months. The CU is a full build of Exchange 2016 and if you are installing a new server you can go with the latest CU (CU15 as of writing this) and you do not need to install RTM and then go to CU1 and then CU2 etc. to get to the latest one. With each build though, you will need to see what the .NET Framework requirements are as mentioned in the .NET Framework section but also the new additional prerequisites required for the Cumulative Update.

Each Cumulative Update has the fixes in from previous ones. So any fixes in CU14 for example is included in CU15. Something to take note of is that if you are on an earlier version of Exchange, say CU10, you won't be able to download CU11 or CU12 as Microsoft only generally keep 2 versions of Cumulative Updates online. If you need to get a copy of an earlier CU, you will need to reach out to Microsoft or your TAM.

When logging calls with Microsoft for an issue, they will generally advise you to upgrade to the latest Cumulative Update and see if it addresses the issue.

Running installation of Cumulative Updates generally is quite a straight forward task. If you prefer using the **Graphical User Interface (GUI)** then you can double click the setup in the large ISO file and navigate through the options and it will advise you that you will do an upgrade if you are upgrading or it will be a full installation if you do an installation from scratch.

You can also run the Cumulative Update in unattended mode and run a simple command to do the upgrade without using the GUI installation. This will be covered in *Chapter 2: Installation of Exchange 2016*.

Conclusion

In this chapter, we discussed Exchange 2016 and what is new compared to other versions. We also looked at all the requirements and prerequisites for Exchange as well as a brief introduction to IISCrypto and locking down your Server. In the next chapter, we will look at performing an installation of Exchange 2016 using the GUI as well as unattended installation.

Questions

Here are some questions to test your knowledge.

1. **In Exchange 2016 you are required to create a public folder database?**

   Answer: No, public folders in Exchange 2016 are now a mailbox.

2. **You need to install a new Exchange 2016 server, which statement is true below:**

   a. Download the latest Cumulative update and run the installation?

   b. Download the RTM version of Exchange 2016 and then update it to each CU till you reach the latest one?

   Answer: a. you can download the latest CU as it is a full version of Exchange 2016.

3. Exchange 2016 consists of 5 roles? Select true or false below:

   a. True

   b. False

   Answer b: Exchange 2016 only has 2 roles.

CHAPTER 2

Installation of Exchange 2016

In this chapter, we will go through the steps to install Exchange 2016 in your environment. We will look at the Virtual Machine preparation and installing all the prerequisites as well as tweaking your network settings.

Structure

The topics covered in this chapter are:

- VM Preparation (includes DNS config, locking down the machine, WINS, Page File)
- Configuring Network Cards.
- IPv6 and IPv4
- Installation of .NET Framework (versions to be explained)
- Installation of prerequisites using PowerShell
- Installation of UCMA 4.0 & Visual C++ 2013
- Installation of Exchange 2016 GUI vs. unattended mode.

Objectives

- Build your virtual machine that will be used for Exchange 2016
- Configure your networks
- Install the prerequisites for Exchange 2016
- Install Exchange 2016 using 2 methods.

Virtual Machine (VM) preparation

Getting your VM ready for Exchange should not be a rushed job. Once you have Exchange installed, you cannot go and do changes or delete the VM without disrupting users.

If you are managing a large organization and will be building machines regularly, you need to prepare a template. This means that you install all your windows updates and configure your network card settings and tune the Operating System for best performance and once you are done with everything you can then run sysprep with the generalize option to ensure you don't end up with duplicate SIDS in Active Directory.

In the topics we mentioned the following:

- DNS config
- WINS config
- Machine lockdown.
- Advanced system settings.

Your DNS config should include 2x of your Domain Controllers. More than that won't be used and we have seen where a machine stops responding with more than 2x IP Addresses.

WINS config, this is something we have been tuning for a while because of the LLMNR requests coming from the machine (Symantec AV throws this out).

In *Figure 2.1* below you can see the settings updated on the machine. This is not a must but if you want to tune your system you can run this config:

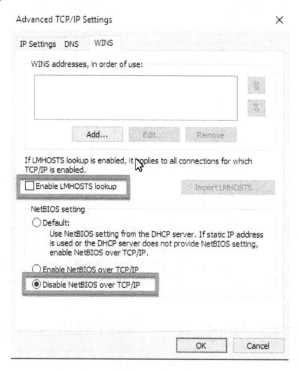

Figure 2.1: *TCP/IP Settings*

Machine lockdown is a big topic. In *Chapter 1: Introduction to Exchange 2016* we spoke about removing older protocols and ciphers using IISCrypto. With the risk of Ransomware out there and most platforms moving away from TLS 1.0 and TLS 1.1 it is advisable to configure your server to only allow TLS 1.2.

The next thing you can do is configure your HTTP Response Headers, this needs to be done on the default website in **IIS (Internet Information Systems).** You will find HTTP Response Headers by default with 1 value in, you can now add the second one as per *Figure 2.2* below:

Figure 2.2: Http Response Headers

The next thing we will tune is the **Advanced Settings.** You can access this by right-clicking on the Start button and choosing **System | Advanced System Settings.** On the system properties page click the **Advanced** tab and then under **Performance** click the **Settings** button.

In *Figure 2.3*, we will configure the Visual Effects as per below:

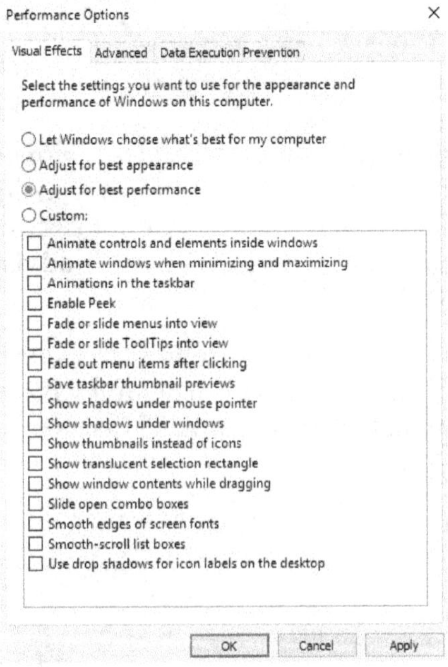

Figure 2.3: Performance options

Don't click **OK** yet, click on the **Advanced** tab and then select **Programs** as per *Figure 2.4*:

Figure 2.4: *Performance Options*

The settings are still not done. You will notice that the page file is large in the image above. This is because we assigned a 40 GB disk to the VM and set the **Page File** to the new disk and took it off the C:\ drive. The setting is generally **32GB + 10MB** as the setting.

Configuring VM network cards

While deep-diving into removing *non-essentials* on the network cards and to fine-tune them, the following can be configured:

- Removing protocols on the Network Card/s
- Enabling RSS (Receive Side Scaling)
- Enabling Rx Ring #1, #2, and Small Rx Buffers.

In *Figure 2.5* below you will see that the following protocols were removed:

- Link Layer (2 of them)
- Multiplexer

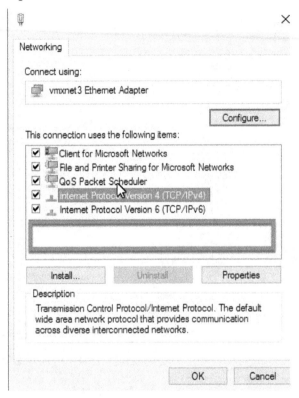

Figure 2.5: Networking properties

Once you have configured the networking, click **OK** to save the changes. Now head back there and click on the **Configure** button.

Once done click on the **Advanced** tab on the new window. This will be where we enable RSS as shown in *Figure 2.6:*

Figure 2.6: *RSS settings*

RSS gives you better performance on the Network card/s. While on the **Advanced** tab, you can scroll down to where it shows **Rx Ring #1 Size** as shown in *Figure 2.7:*

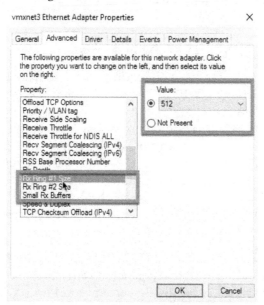

Figure 2.7: *Rx Ring Settings*

We set these to 512 and have not kept the default of **Not Present.** A word of caution here. This does increase latency, so you need to adjust this to your needs or leave it default.

IPv4 and IPv6

This is generally a big topic to discuss because of the fact the way that IT Admins disable IPv6 and cause issues on the Exchange Server. The first common mistake is deselecting the tick box next to IPv6 on the system properties and rebooting. This causes the machine to become unresponsive and hang most of the time.

The best way to **disable** IPv6 is to run the command in PowerShell and then reboot. This removes the tick box the safe way. The next debate here is that they say you should keep IPv6 enabled for Exchange. We have worked in environments with it enabled and disabled and have not seen any issues either way however Microsoft recommends leaving it enabled on the Windows Server Operating System.

> ****A side from security note, we have seen Malware tunnel from IPv4 to IPv6 when it's enabled. For example, if the Gateway has been taken out of a server that does not need internet access, the Malware will use IPv6 to tunnel to another server which does have internet access to download files or do mining, etc. ****

Installation of .NET Framework

.NET Framework has been a requirement for Exchange from the early days. Exchange 2010 was a big one and when new versions of .NET Framework came out, IT admins made the mistakes of installing them which resulted in virtual directories not working and strange events happening on Exchange. You will notice in the support matrix that Microsoft has online, only certain versions of Exchange like Exchange 2016 CU13 or Exchange 2019 CU2 support .NET 4.8. Older versions will support .NET 4.7.1 or .NET 4.7.2 but no version supports .NET 4.7 and they warn you about installing it on your Exchange server.

Other times WSUS servers or **SCCM (System Center Configuration Manager)** pushes the updates if approved to servers and this is also where it causes an issue. Be certain you know what version is required and support with your version of Exchange Server.

The download for .NET 4.8 in this example is not a big file 100 MB and can be downloaded as an offline installer. Below are the screenshots of the installation. *Figure 2.8,* running the install file you downloaded begins with extracting the files:

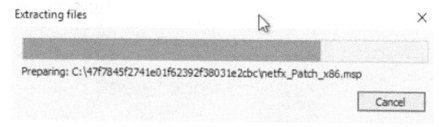

Figure 2.8: .NET Framework Setup

Figure 2.9 below, you need to accept the license terms to use the software:

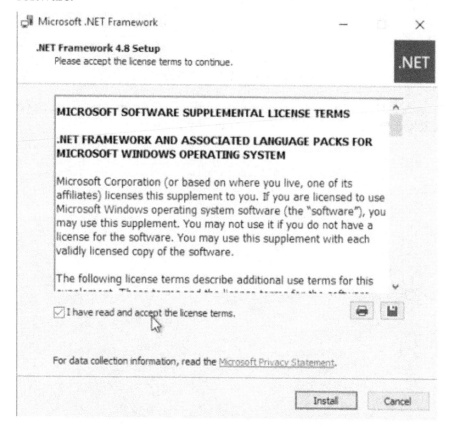

Figure 2.9: .NET Framework Setup

Figure 2.10, after you click install you can monitor the progress of the install as shown below:

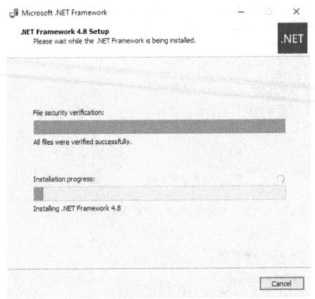

Figure 2.10: *.NET Framework Setup*

Figure 2.11, installation is complete on the last screen. Once you have clicked **Finish** you will need to reboot your server:

Figure 2.11: *.NET Framework Setup*

Once your installation is complete, click the **Finish** button. The setup will prompt you to reboot your server. Click **Yes** to reboot and then proceed to the next section.

Installation of prerequisites for the role you want to install on your 2016 Windows Server

Exchange 2016 just like Exchange 2010 or Exchange 2013 or Exchange 2019 requires different roles/features to be installed on the server before you can install Exchange. As we are dealing with Exchange 2016 in this book, there are only 2 roles you can install, this is the Exchange 2016 Mailbox role or the Exchange 2016 Edge role.

You no longer have the ability to install the Client Access role or Hub transport role as Microsoft changed the architecture in Exchange 2013. Exchange 2016 followed that architecture. The following needs to be installed on both servers:

- .NET 4.X (See what Microsoft require for the CU you want to install)
- UCMA 4.0 Runtime
- PowerShell Prerequisites.

To install the prerequisites for the Mailbox role you need to run the following from an elevated PowerShell window:

Install-WindowsFeature NET-Framework-45-Features, RPC-over-H TTP-proxy, RSAT-Clustering, RSAT-Clustering-CmdInterface, RSAT-Clustering-Mgmt, RSAT-Clustering-PowerShell, Web-Mgmt-Console, WAS-Process-Model, Web-Asp-Net45, Web-Basic-Auth, Web-Client-Auth, Web-Digest-Auth, Web-Dir-Browsing, Web-Dyn-Compression, Web-Http-Errors, Web-Http-Logging, Web-Http-Redirect, Web-Http-Tracing, Web-ISAPI-Ext, Web-ISAPI-Filter, Web-Lgcy-Mgmt-Console, Web-Metabase, Web-Mgmt-Console, Web-Mgmt-Service, Web-Net-Ext45, Web-Request-Monitor, Web-Server, Web-Stat-Compression, Web-Static-Content, Web-Windows-Auth, Web-WMI, Windows-Identity-Foundation, RSAT-ADDS

Below is an example of a PowerShell window running the prerequisites:

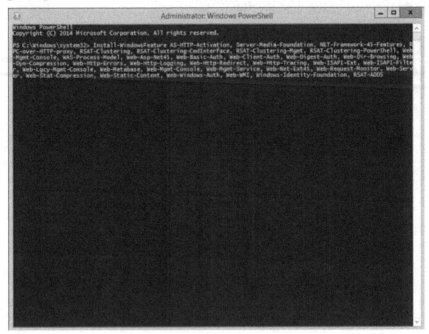

Figure 2.12: PowerShell Prerequisites

For the Edge Role you need to run the following:

`Install-WindowsFeature ADLDS`

As you can see the Edge role has a small set of requirements vs. a Mailbox Server installation.

Installation of UCMA 4.0

Exchange 2016 which is the final version to have the feature/role Unified messaging, you need to install unified communications manager API 4.0. Your Exchange 2016 setup will not work if you do not install this. Once you have done your installation you then need to reboot the server before attempting the installation of Exchange 2016.

Below is what the setup screens look like:

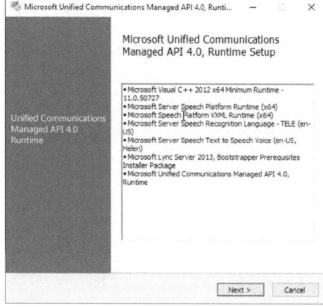

Figure 2.13: UCMA Setup

Click **Next** to start the installation of UCMA 4.0. Accept the license terms and then click the `Install` button:

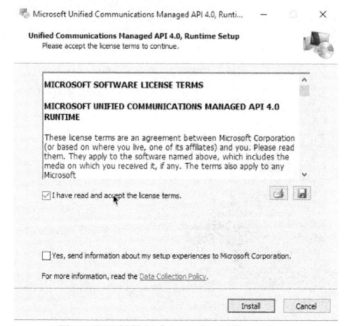

Figure 2.14: UCMA Setup – Accept license terms

Below is a progress screen of the installation. Depending on how powerful your server is this can take a few minutes or longer.

Figure 2.15: UCMA Setup

The setup installs Visual C++ 2012 and then proceeds with UCMA 4.0. The installation of UCMA 4.0 has completed. Click the **Finish** button and reboot your server to continue with the other installations:

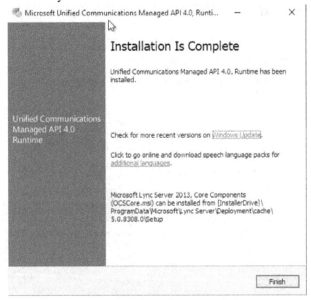

Figure 2.16: UCMA Setup completion

Below is the setup for the Visual C++ 2013 installation. Agree to the license terms and then the **Install** button will highlight and let you install:

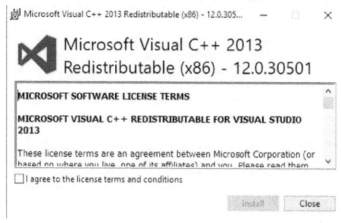

Figure 2.17: Visual C++ Installation

The installation completes quite quickly, once done you can click the **Finish/Close** button and reboot your server before starting with your Exchange 2016 installation.

Installation of Exchange 2016

You need to ensure that the account you are using to run the installation is part of the Domain, Schema, and Enterprise Admins Groups

Launch the setup file located in the ISO you downloaded elevated and wait for the setup to start. You will need to check for updates and accept the license terms before proceeding below:

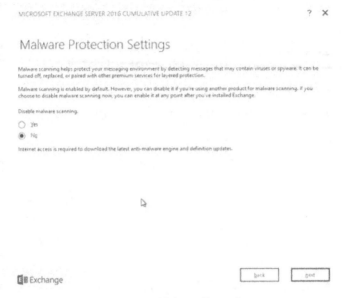

Figure 2.18: *Malware Protection*

In the **Malware Protection Settings** screen shown above, leave the default and click **next**:

Figure 2.19: *Readiness Checks*

Once the readiness checks have completed, the install button will become active allowing you to proceed. Click **install**.

Step 1 below performs an organization prep, meaning it runs the setup with the /PrepareAD switch in the background:

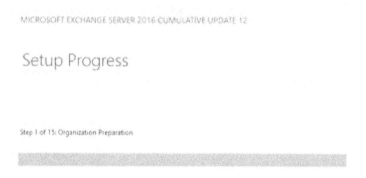

Figure 2.20: Setup Progress

The setup now stops services to proceed with the installation:

Figure 2.21: Exchange 2016 Setup – Stopping Services

In step 3, the setup copies files to the server. This process can take some time and it might look like its stuck at 16% but just wait for it to finish:

Figure 2.22: Exchange 2016 Setup – Copy Exchange Files

The setup now run **Language Files:**

Figure 2.23: Exchange 2016 Setup – Language Files

The setup now restores all services to continue with the setup:

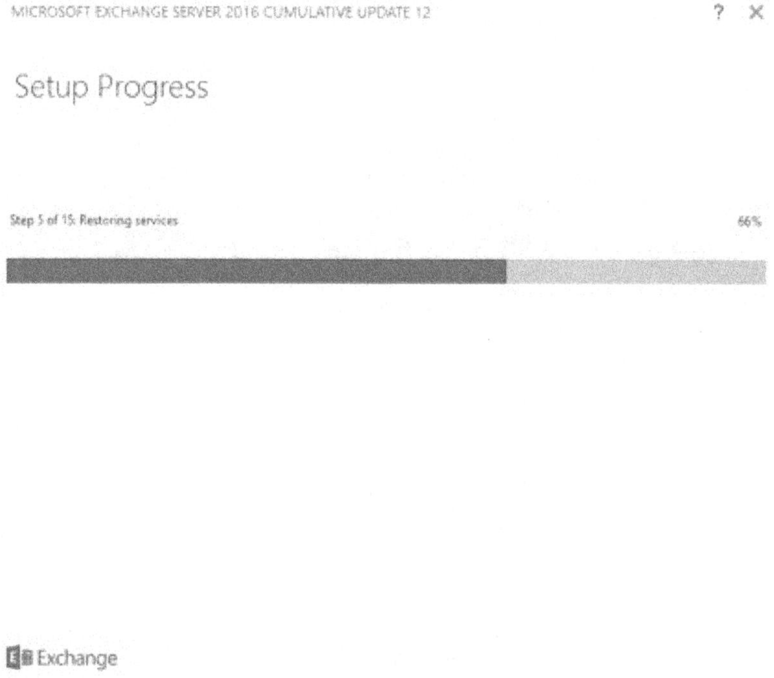

MICROSOFT EXCHANGE SERVER 2016 CUMULATIVE UPDATE 12   ?   ✕

Setup Progress

Step 5 of 15: Restoring services   66%

E⬛ Exchange

Figure 2.24*: Exchange 2016 Setup – Restoring Services*

Next, the management tools are installed:

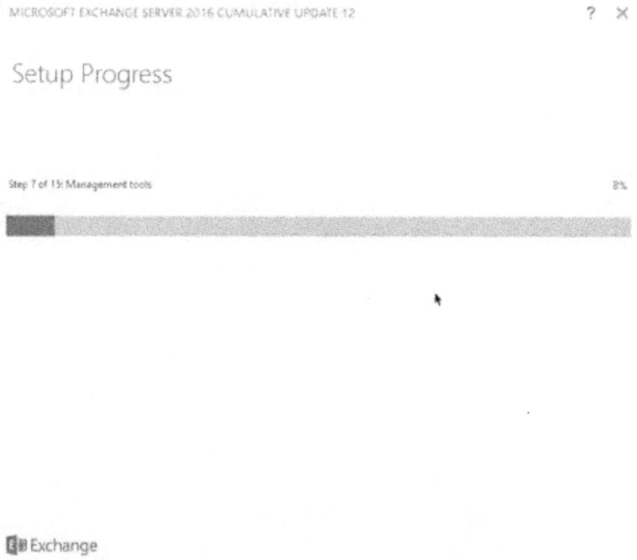

MICROSOFT EXCHANGE SERVER 2016 CUMULATIVE UPDATE 12   ?   ✕

Setup Progress

Step 7 of 15: Management tools   8%

E⬛ Exchange

Figure 2.25*: Exchange 2016 Setup – Management Tools*

The setup is now installing the **Transport service:**

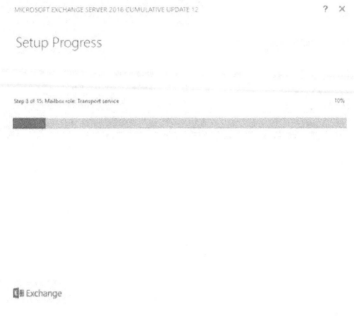

Figure 2.26: *Exchange 2016 Setup – Mailbox Role: Transport Service*

Setup is now installing the **Client Access service:**

Figure 2.27: *Exchange 2016 Setup – Mailbox role: Client Access Service*

Setup is installing the **Unified Messaging service:**

Figure 2.28: *Exchange 2016 Setup – Unified Messaging.*

Setup is installing the **Mailbox service:**

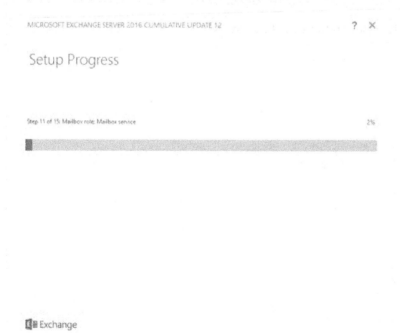

Figure 2.29: *Exchange 2016 Setup – Mailbox Role: Mailbox Service*

The setup is installing the **Front End Transport service:**

Figure 2.30: *Exchange 2016 Setup – Mailbox Role: Front End Transport Service*

Setup is installing the **Client Access Front End service:**

Figure 2.31: *Exchange 2016 Setup – Mailbox Role: Client Access Front End Service*

This is the final piece of the installation. Exchange 2016 setup is finalizing the setup:

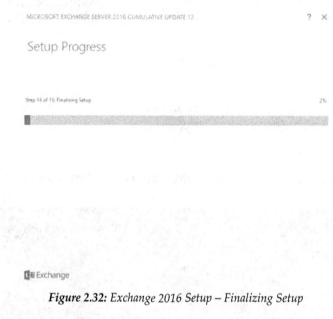

Figure 2.32: *Exchange 2016 Setup – Finalizing Setup*

The setup has completed. You can tick the box below to open the Exchange Admin Center but it is advisable to reboot the server first before carrying on:

Figure 2.33: *Exchange 2016 Setup Completed.*

The setup is pretty straight forward. Below we will take a look at doing the setup again but this time unattended. You still need to follow the same process of installing the prerequisites and .NET, UCMA 4.0, Visual C++ 2013 before doing the installation of Exchange 2016.

Launch an elevated Command Prompt on the server and run the following command:

Setup.exe   /IAcceptExchangeServerLicenseTerms   / Mode:Install /Roles:Mailbox

Or you can use this command:

.\Setup.exe /IAcceptExchangeServerLicenseTerms /m:Install /R:MB

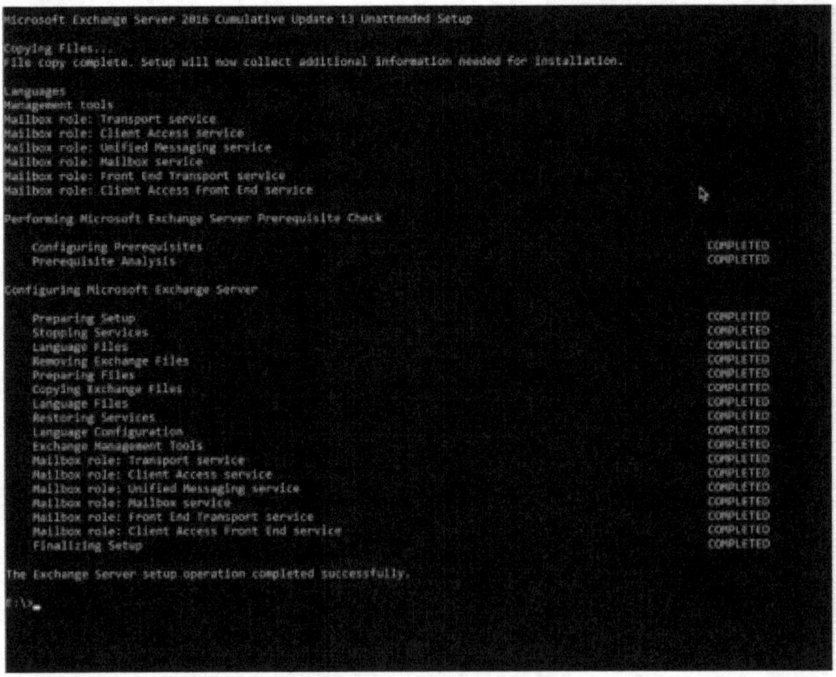

Figure 2.34: Unatte nded Setup of Exchange 2016

As you can see the installation is cleaner than the GUI installation and much easier to run. Some IT Admins prefer the GUI methods, others prefer the Unattended one.

Conclusion

To conclude, in this chapter we took a look at preparing our Virtual Machine for Exchange 2016. We configured the network cards and ran through all the prerequisites. We took a look at what a GUI install looks like vs. an unattended install. In the next chapter, we will perform post configurations of our server.

Questions

1. **I can run the installation of Exchange 2016 without running anything else?**

    Answer: Incorrect, you need to install the prerequisites for Exchange 2016 as well as UCMA 4.0 Runtime, Visual C++ and .NET

2. **I can launch the Exchange Admin Center after my installation and carry on configuring my server?**

    Answer: Yes you can, however, it is advisable to reboot first for all the changes to take effect.

CHAPTER 3

Post Configuration of Exchange 2016

Exchange 2016 running without config will work, you can login to Outlook on the Web (OWA) and you can launch the Exchange Admin Center but if you try and access it externally you won't be able to. Configuration of Exchange 2016 is essential because you need to define you send connector and update your receive connectors to accept mail from the internet as well as add in your accepted domains. You also need to license your server as you will only be able to mount a certain number of databases and you do not want to be running on a trial version.

If you forget to configure your URLs and have a valid SSL certificate in place you will get popups on outlook and clients will not be very happy. In the previous chapter, we completed our Exchange 2016 Installation and in this chapter, we will look at performing post configurations. We explain the Exchange Admin Center in detail.

Structure

The topics covered in this chapter are:

- Launching the Exchange Admin Center (EAC) – Explanation of all tabs.

- Launching the Exchange Management Shell (EMS)
- Server Licensing (Standard vs Enterprise)
- Send Connector creation/configuration
- Receive connector explanation and configuration
- Setup Journaling

Objectives

- Launch the Exchange Admin Center and understand each tab on the left.
- Launch the Exchange Management Shell and run commands.
- License your Exchange 2016 Server.
- Setup your connectors.
- Configure the journal for your environment.

Launching the Exchange Admin Center (EAC) – Explanation of all tabs

Once you have Exchange 2016 installed, you can manage it in 2 ways. Using the **Exchange Admin Center (EAC)** which has limited functionality and using the **Exchange Management Shell (EMS)** which we will cover next in this chapter. If you click the start button on your Windows Server 2016 machine and expand the Microsoft Exchange 2016 folder, you can then click on the Exchange Admin Center and it will launch a web browser.

To access this you can use the URL on your Exchange 2016 Server:

`https://localhost/owa`

If you want to access it from another machine in the network and you are running Exchange 2010 coexistence then you can use the following URL:

`https://MailboxServer1/ecp/?ExchClientVer=15`

As you can see it has the `ClientVer=15` at the end. If you fail to have this in the URL it will redirect you to the Exchange 2010 ECP if you are running coexistence. Once launched you will get a login screen as shown below in *Figure 3.1:*

Figure 3.1: Exchange Admin Center

Enter in your admin account details, for example, `domain\admin_ account` and the password. It will take a few minutes to login and then you should see a screen similar to the one below in *Figure 3.2:*

Figure 3.2: Exchange Admin Center - Servers

From within the Exchange Admin Center, you have the following tabs:

- Recipients
- Permissions
- Compliance Management
- Organization
- Protection
- Mail Flow
- Mobile
- Public Folders
- Unified Messaging
- Servers
- Hybrid

Let's take a look at what you can do under each of these as they have multiple options.

Recipients

Figure 3.3 shows the main tab with its subtabs you can work on:

recipients   mailboxes   groups   resources   contacts   shared   migration

Figure 3.3: Recipients

This allows you to view/configure the following:

- **mailboxes**: You can view the current mailboxes in the organization as well as create a new user or linked mailbox.
- **groups**: Allows you to view the current groups and create new ones.
- **resources**: This is where you can view your current resource mailboxes and create new ones.
- **contacts**: Here you can view the current contacts saved in the environment and also create new ones.
- **shared**: This is where your shared mailboxes are shown and you can create new ones.
- **migration**: This is where you can create a migration batch of mailboxes to move from one database to another database.

Permissions

Figure 3.4, under permissions you can set the roles and polices as shown below:

Figure 3.4: Permissions

This allows you to view/configure the following:

- **admin roles:** When you install Exchange it creates a list of security groups in Active Directory which you can manage from both AD and Exchange. Here is where you can assign permissions to users. For example, if you want somebody to only work on the Help Desk role then you can add them to this role. They won't be able to do big tasks like create DAG's, etc. but they can assist with account creations, etc.

- **user roles**: This is where you can create new policies that you want to assign to users.

- **Outlook Web App policies:** This allows you to create policies and assign to users, for example, you don't want the finance department changing themes, and then you can remove that option for them.

Compliance management

Figure 3.5 below is where you can set in-place hold for legal purposes or check audit reports etc.

in-place eDiscovery & hold   auditing   data loss prevention   retention policies   retention tags   journal rules

Figure 3.5: Compliance management

This allows you to configure the following options:

- **in-place eDiscovery & hold:** You can create a search to find specific things in user mailboxes, you need to be added to the security group to be able to do these searches.

- **auditing:** This allows you to view audit logs, but take note **You need to enable the audit log first to be able to pull information**

- **data loss prevention:** Here you can configure DLP policies for what to do with sensitive information, like sending a copy of the email to a manager when it contains the words *credit card* as an example.

- **retention policies:** A retention policy allows you to define what to do with email. For example, create a TAG to archive all emails over a certain period or move mail to an archive mailbox.

- **retention tags:** Retention policies are applied by creating TAG's as mentioned above.

- **journal rules:** This allows you to create a journal rule to define what to do with all company email or what to do with a user's email, etc.

Organization

Figure 3.6 shown below is where you can set up federation and apps that will be available to users and view your address lists:

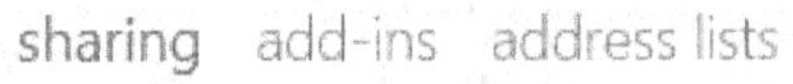

sharing   add-ins   address lists

Figure 3.6: Organization

This allows you to setup/view the following:

- **sharing**: This is where you can setup a federation trust. For example, if company A buys company B they can do sharing while they transition to either a new forest or to either one of them.

- **apps/add-ins**: From here you can add add-ins for users to use in outlook and you can assign this to everyone or specific users/groups.

- **address lists**: This is where you can view your current address lists like the default address list and all rooms, groups and contacts, etc. You can also add new Address lists from here.

Protection

Figure 3.7 shows you the malware filter that you either left enable in setup or disabled and you can import other filters as well:

malware filter

Figure 3.7: *Malware Filter*

When you run the setup for Exchange 2016 there was a section for Protection. You either chose to leave the default and enable the malware filter or disable it. Here you can add additional anti-malware policies.

Mail Flow

Figure 3.8 is the main section where you add in your domains and configure you connectors for mail flow:

rules   delivery reports   accepted domains   email address policies   receive connectors   send connectors

Figure 3.8: *Mail Flow*

In this section you can configure the following:

- **rules**: Here you can create new Transport Rules that will be applied to emails in the organization.

- **delivery reports**: Here is where you can search a mailbox for messages

- **accepted domain**: You need to create an accepted domain like domain.com to be able to send/receive mail.

- **email address policies**: A default policy is assigned to everyone in the organization, if you have different organizational units, you can create policies for each one.

- **receive connectors**: You need a receive connector to be able to receive mail from the internet. In exchange 2016 it should work out the box and it is advisable to not fiddle with the original connectors but create new ones for applications or printers.

- **send connectors**: You define a send connector and specify if you want to send mail using DNS or a smart host to the internet. You can also specify one or all your servers to be able to send mail.

Mobile

Figure 3.9 below shows you what you can configure for ActiveSync devices:

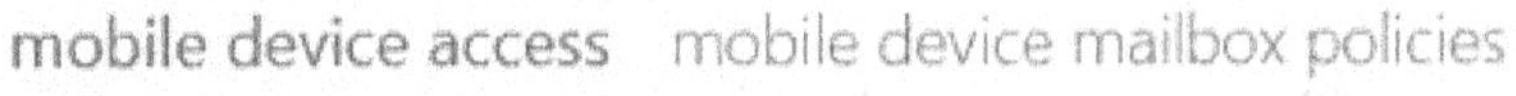

mobile device access   mobile device mailbox policies

Figure 3.9: Mobile

In this section you can configure/view the following:

- **Mobile device access**: Here you can view any quarantined devices and also setup device access rules or view rules in place already.

- **Mobile device mailbox policies**: A default policy is assigned here but you can create a new one as per the requirements of the organization.

Public Folders

Figure 3.10 below is where you can configure your public folder mailbox and folders:

public folders   public folder mailboxes

Figure 3.10: Public folders

In Exchange 2016, you no longer have a public folder database but you have a public folder mailbox which makes it highly available when you run a DAG.

In this section you can configure/view the following:

- **public folders**: Here you can create public folders you want to assign to a folder.

- **public folder mailboxes:** This allows you to create public folder mailboxes and assign permissions of who can access them.

Unified messaging

Figure 3.11 below is where you can set up your dial plans and gateways:

UM dial plans   UM IP gateways

Figure 3.11: Unified Messaging

In this section you can configure the following:

- **UM dial plans**: You use this to manage UM features for a group of users who are enabled for voice mail.
- **UM IP gateways:** An IP Gateway links UM to a physical IP gateway device you have on your premises.

Servers

Figure 3.12 below is where you will configure you DAG and virtual directories as well as licensing your servers and configuring your certificates:

servers databases database availability groups virtual directories certificates

Figure 3.12: Servers

This is what I call the main section as here you can view/configure the following:

- **servers**: Here you can view your servers and you can license them, configure POP/IMAP settings, Configure Outlook Anywhere as well as DNS Lookups, Transport Limits, and logs.
- **databases:** Here you can view the current databases you have and also create new ones. You can enable circular logging and remove the default database exchange creates when you run the install.
- **database availability groups**: In this section, you can view any current DAG's you have as well as create a new DAG and modify group membership and assign IP addresses.
- **virtual directories:** In this section, you can configure your URLs that exchange will use for OWA, ECP, AS, OAB,

and PowerShell. You can also specify your authentication methods to use.

- **certificates:** Here you can view the status of your current SSL certificate as well as create a new certificate request or import an SSL certificate as well as export an SSL Certificate.

Hybrid

Figure 3.13 below gives you the option to configure a hybrid connection with Office 365:

Figure 3.13: Hybrid

If your organization will be making use of Office 365, you can configure Hybrid from here and you will need to login to your tenant in Office 365 before you run the Hybrid Configuration Wizard.

Launching the Exchange Management Shell (EMS)

In the first section, we spoke about the **Exchange Admin Center (EAC)** and how you can configure certain things using a web browser (GUI). You can do everything in the **Exchange Management Shell (EMS)** that the EAC can do and more. Remember the EAC runs Powershell commands in the background. To launch the EMS, you can click on the start menu, expand Microsoft Exchange Server 2016, and right-click on the Exchange Management Shell and launch it as administrator.

This is what it will look like once it has loaded all the cmdlets as shown in *Figure 3.14* below:

Figure 3.14: *Exchange Management Shell*

In some organizations, this is all you will have to work with as the Exchange Admin Center might be disabled due to its surface attack. In an example, if you wanted to view all the Mailbox Databases within the organization, you could run the following command:

Get-MailboxDatabaseCopyStatus *

Once you have run the command you will see a similar window as shown in *Figure 3.15* below:

Figure 3.15: *Exchange Management Shell*

There are many other commands you can run. If you add users to groups other than the Org Management Group they might not be able to run this as it will come back and say the command is not recognized.

Server Licensing (Standard vs. Enterprise)

In Exchange 2016, you have the option to license your server in 2 Editions:

- Standard Edition
- Enterprise Edition

Now, remember you can install any **Cumulative Update (CU)** of Exchange 2016 and it will be a fully operational server however in trial mode you are limited to the number of databases you can create. If you are a small organization, you might lean towards Standard Edition but with this version, you can only create a maximum of 5 databases and no more.

If you are planning to have multiple DAG's and multiple databases, you can look at Enterprise Edition as this will give you up to 100 mounted mailbox databases.

Send connector creation/ configuration

To be able to send emails to the internet, you most likely will have an ISP you sending to like Mimecast, Symantec, RocketSeed to name a few. They will give you a smart host that you will enter into the configuration of your Send Connector. Remember, you need to have MX records created externally in DNS so other domains know about you and how to get to you.

In the Exchange Admin Center, you can go to Mail Flow and then click on Send Connectors on the top right. If you are running coexistence, you will see your current send connectors, however, if this is a new

Forest and Domain you will have to set it up. Click on the + button to create a new send connector as shown in *Figure 3.16 below:*

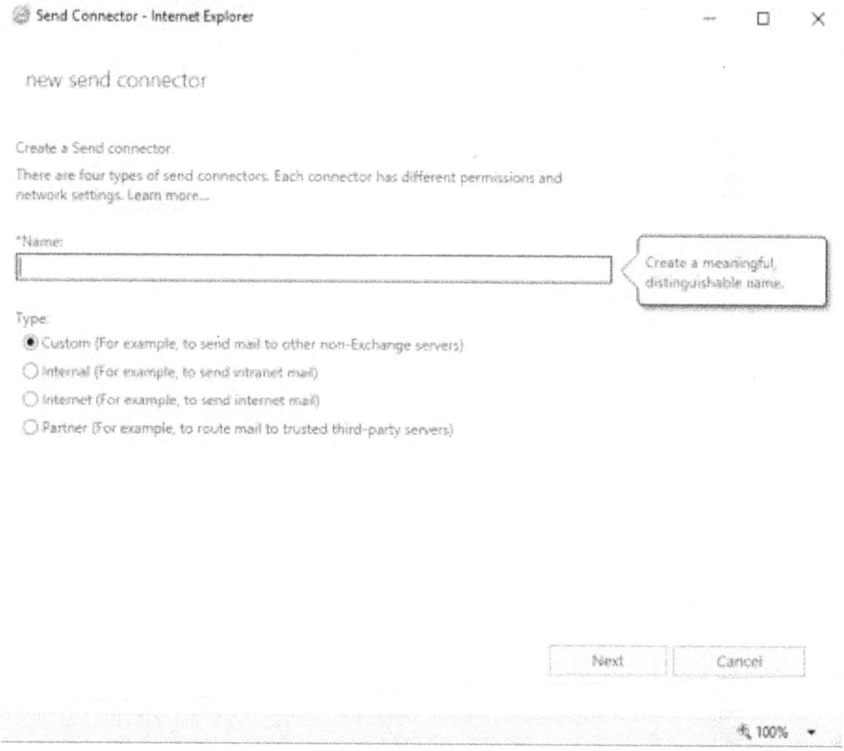

Figure 3.16: Send Connector

Here you need to give your send connector a name and then choose a type. Once done click the **Next** button which will take you to *Figure 3.17* as shown below:

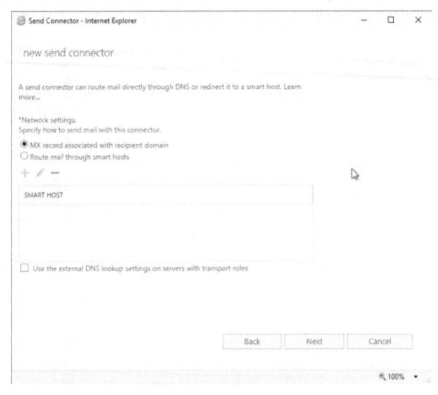

Figure 3.17: Send Connector

In this section, you will choose the section option under network settings to route mail through a smart host and then click the + button again to add in the details as shown in *Figure 3.18* below:

Figure 3.18: Network Settings (Smart host)

Enter in the details your ISP has provided and click **Save**. You will be taken back to the previous screen and your configuration should look similar to *Figure 3.19* below:

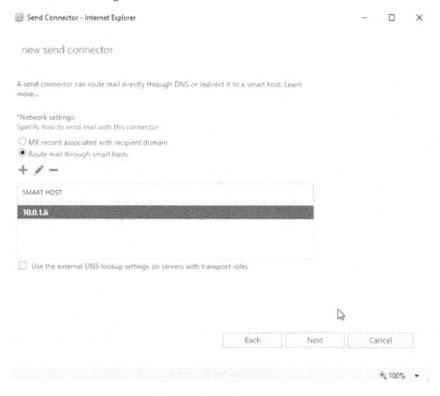

Figure 3.19: Send Connector

As you can see your smart host now has info in and you can click **Next** to continue. In *Figure 3.20* below, you can specify your smart host authentication if your ISP provided you with this or you can leave it as none and click **Next** to continue:

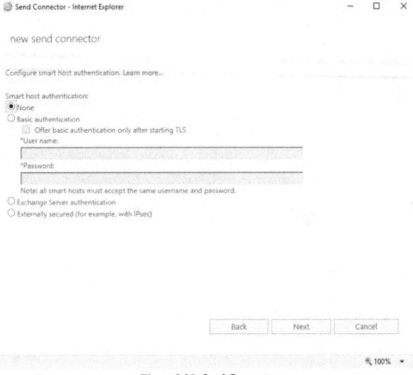

Figure 3.20: *Send Connector*

In *Figure 3.21* shown below, you now need to create an address space. Remember that you won't just have 1 send connector, you might have multiple ones especially if you are a hoster. Click the + button to create your address space:

Figure 3.21: *Send Connector*

In *Figure 3.22* shown below, you need to configure the following:

- **Type:** By default, it is set to SMTP
- **FQDN:** Most will use * but you can enter what is relevant for your company.
- **Cost:** Default is 1.

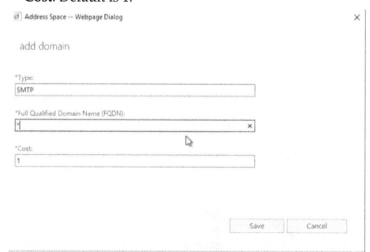

Figure 3.22: *Add Domain*

Once done, click **Save**. You will be taken back to the previous screen where your **Address space** info will now show as per *Figure 3.23* below:

Figure 3.23: Send Connector

Click **Next** to continue. In *Figure 3.24* shown below, you now need to specify which servers are going to handling mail:

Figure 3.24: Send Connector

Click the + button to add to your servers.

A new window will show with the list of servers, select the servers you want and then save it and once you are returned to the previous screen you can click **Finish** to set up your Send Connector. In *Figure 3.25* below you can see the newly created Send connector:

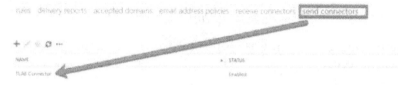

Figure 3.25: *Send Connector.*

Once you click **Finish** in *Figure 3.24*, you will be taken back to the main screen and your new Send connector will show in the list.

Receive connector explanation and configuration

In Exchange 2010, you had two receive connectors, default and client. In Exchange 2016 you have 5 receive connectors. Let's go through each of them in a bit of detail:

Connector Name	Brief Description	TCP Port
Client Frontend <Server>	Accepts connections from authenticated SMTP clients using secure port 587.	587
Default Frontend <Server>	Accepts anonymous connections from External servers. This is the message entry point into your Exchange Environment.	25
Outbound Proxy Frontend <Server>	Accepts authenticated connections from the Transport Service on other mailbox servers.	717
Client Proxy <Server>	Accepts authenticated client connections that are proxied from the FE Transport Service	465

Default <Server>	This connector accepts authenticated connections from the FE Transport service, local and external. Transport service on remote mbx servers.	2525

Table 3.1: Exchange 2016 Connectors

For more information on this, you can read the documentation on Microsoft's website:

https://docs.microsoft.com/en-us/exchange/mail-flow/connectors/receive-connectors?view=exchserver-2019

Setup journaling

Many organizations have Journaling setup. This can be to a journal mailbox or to an external party that filters mail for your organization. Every mail sent and received in the organization is journaled and on the ISP platform, you can do a search for an email when it is required like for a legal case. You get two kinds of journaling options:

- **Standard Journaling**: Standard Journaling journals all messages in the organization to a mailbox on a mailbox database.

- **Premium Journaling:** Premium Journal uses journal rules to journal the organization's mail either on all recipients or selected ones and you can select your scope which is either internal messages or external messages or all messages in the organization. Be aware that you require an Exchange Enterprise CAL for premium journaling.

To setup Journaling in Exchange 2016, you can launch the **Exchange Admin Center (EAC)** and then click on **Compliance. Management** on the left-hand pane and then once you see all the tabs on the right you can click on journal rules. Clicking the + button will allow you to create a journal rule.

You will be presented with a screen as shown in *Figure 3.26* below:

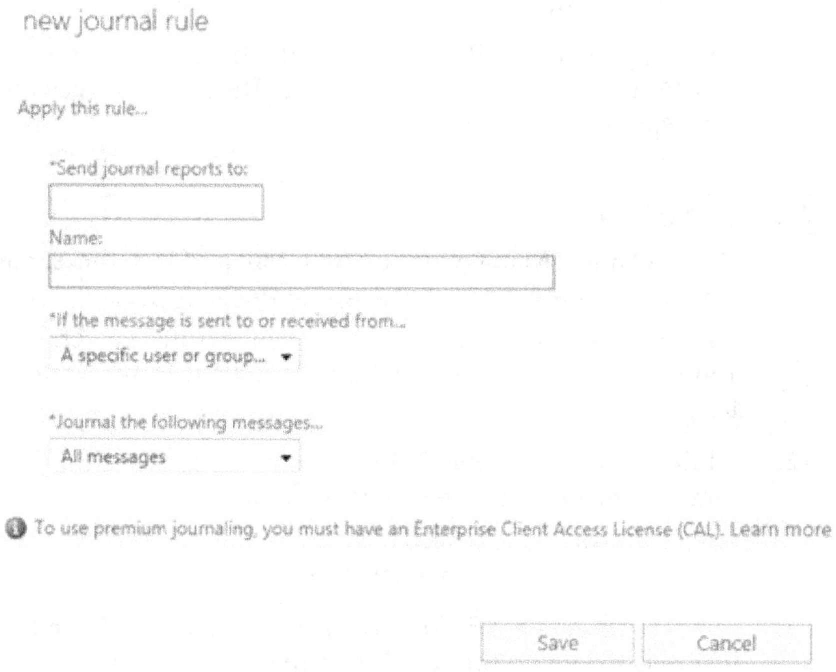

new journal rule

Apply this rule...

*Send journal reports to:

Name:

*If the message is sent to or received from...

A specific user or group... ▼

*Journal the following messages...

All messages ▼

ⓘ To use premium journaling, you must have an Enterprise Client Access License (CAL). Learn more

Save   Cancel

Figure 3.26: *Journal Rule*

Here you can define where the journal reports go to and give this rule a name and then select your conditions from the drop-down list, either a specific user or group as shown above or all users and then select to journal the following messages drop-down. Click **Save** for the rule to be created.

Conclusion

By now you should know your way around the **Exchange Admin Center (EAC)**. You learnt how to firstly view where your mailboxes are located and how to set up and configure your Accepted domains and send/receive connectors and also have a clear understanding of what each receive connector is used for. You also learnt where you can license your servers as well as set up or maintain your **Database Availability Groups (DAG)** and configure your virtual directories so that your clients can connect externally and internally without an error. Lastly, you learnt about Journaling and how to set it up as well as learning that if you want to use the advanced features you need to have an enterprise CAL.

In the next chapter, we will continue with the configuration of Exchange 2016. You will learn how to work in IIS and how to create a certificate request and complete it.

Questions

1. **The Exchange Management Shell can perform the same functions as the Exchange Admin center?**

   Answer: Yes, the Exchange admin center runs PowerShell commands in the background and is limited to what it can do.

2. **If I license my Exchange 2016 server with Standard Edition I am able to add more than 5 databases?**

   Answer: Incorrect, you need to be licensed with the Enterprise edition to add more than 5 databases in Exchange for 2016.

3. **I want to receive email from the internet, what do I need to ensure is ticked on the Receive connector?**

   Answer: You need to ensure that anonymous is enabled on the default frontend connector.

CHAPTER 4

Post Configuration Continued

Security is a big thing today and to ensure you have a secure URL to access Outlook on the Web (OWA) you need to purchase an SSL certificate and use this certificate on your Exchange 2016 server. The URLs you define in Exchange need to be resolvable on the internet so your certificate needs to have those names on and Exchange 2016 needs to be configured using them so you have smooth connectivity with your clients that connect with different protocols. If there is a problem with the certificate or it expires, the end-user will feel the pain the most with a constant popup, etc.

In this chapter, you will learn how to create your first certificate request and how to complete it as well as understanding how you can import a .PFX file into IIS. You will also learn how to work with **Internet Information Systems (IIS)** to configure your bindings. If the wrong certificate is chosen on the bindings, then OWA or Outlook will give errors. Before we start with the Certificate section, let's talk a bit about certificates. Exchange Admins find this one a bit more tricky to configure but shouldn't as it is straight forward to do.

Structure

- Certificates – Creating a CSR and installing the SSL certificate.
- Certificates – Exporting/Importing PFX file directly into IIS.
- Certificates – Configuring IIS Bindings to use your new SSL certificate.
- Virtual Directories – Configuring your virtual directories.

Objectives

- Work with SSL certificates.
- Configure and view bindings.
- Edit your virtual directories.

Exchange certificates

What do certificates do and why do I need it? Firstly, you want to ensure the safety and security of the systems you expose to the internet so having a valid SSL Certificate, whether it is a SAN Certificate or a Wildcard Certificate, it will have your domain information on.

On your Exchange 2016 server, you will bind IIS to the certificate which we will cover later on in this chapter.

I have an internal CA, why do I need to purchase an expensive SSL certificate? It is all fair and well having an internal CA do your certificates, however, the certificate won't be trusted on the internet and your site will be listed as vulnerable. If you didn't expose Exchange 2016 to the internet and only used it for internal purposes then that will be a different thing altogether.

Your virtual directories which will be covered later on in this chapter needs to be configured to match what your certificate has on it. For example, if you use a common name like `mail.thexchangelab.com`, I can configure all my URL's to use this namespace and I will use `Autodiscover.thexchangelab.com` for my Autodiscover URL. However, the certificate needs to be accessible from outside along with the certificate authority. Digicert, RapidSSL, Godaddy are just some of the trusted vendors that do SSL certificates.

Can I use my SSL Certificate on multiple servers? Yes, you can. If you have installed your new SSL Certificate on your first Exchange 2016 server, you can simply export it and import it into the next server.

What about my load balancers/firewalls? You need to install your SSL certificate on them as they are internet facing. If you do not install it you will get popups on your outlook clients with the load balancer default certificate which you don't want.

Let's take a look at the options for creating/importing certificates below.

Creating a CSR and installing the SSL certificate

Login to the **Exchange Admin Center (EAC)** and then click on Servers on the left-hand side and then click on **Certificates** on the top right as shown in *Figure 4.1*:

Figure 4.1: *Certificates*

Click the + button to create a new Exchange Certificate, once done it will bring up a new window as shown in *Figure 4.2* below:

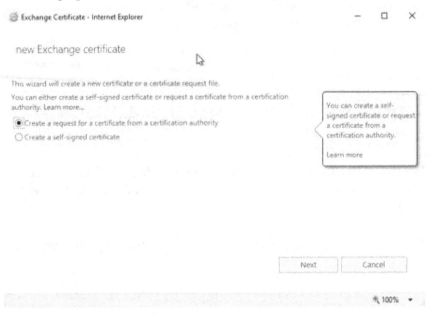

Figure 4.2: *New Exchange Certificate*

In the window above leave the default to **Create a request for a certificate from a certification authority** and then click **Next**:

Figure 4.3: *New Exchange Certificate Friendly name*

In *Figure 4.3* list above, you need to give a friendly name for your certificate and then click **Next**. In *Figure 4.4* shown below if you want to use a Wildcard certificate then select the box above or leave it to default and then click **Next**.

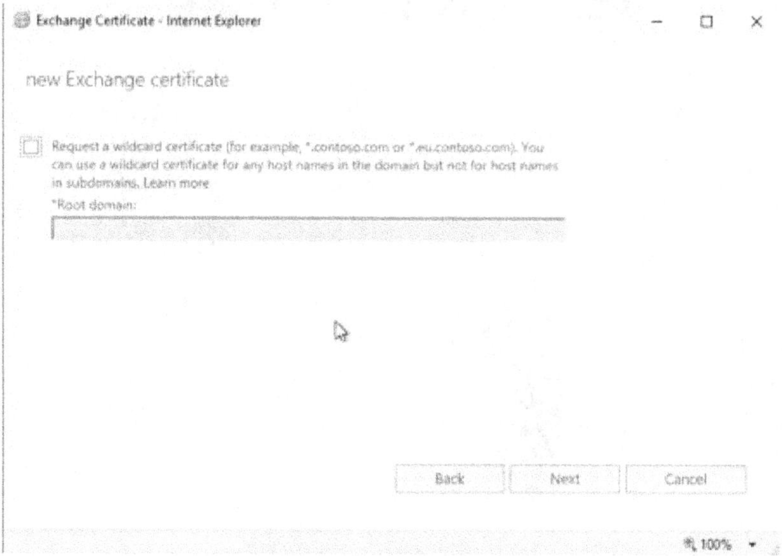

Figure 4.4: *Request a WildCard*

In *Figure 4.5* shown below, you need to select a server and then click **Browse**.

Figure 4.5: *Certificate request placement*

This will bring up *Figure 4.6* as shown below:

Figure 4.6: *Select a Server*

Once you have selected your server, click **OK** to be taken back to the previous screen where it will show your server you selected as in *Figure 4.7* below:

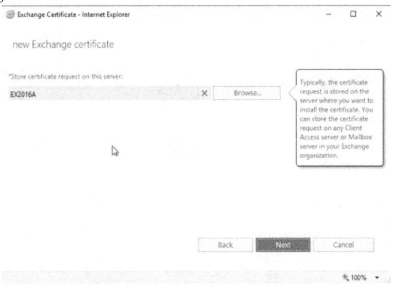

Figure 4.7: *Store Certificate with Server Name*

Now click **Next**. In *Figure 4.8* below, you need to edit the different URLs and enter in the domain name. In this example, I have used `mail.thexchangelab.com`. Scroll down to enter information for POP/IMAP/Outlook Anywhere and then click **Next**:

Figure 4.8: Configure your domains

In *Figure 4.9* shown below, you need to take note of the fact that you cannot include internal server names or domain names. In *Figure 4.8* you need to remove internal names like *`.local` where * will be your internal domain name:

Figure 4.9: Domains

As you can see above, I am using `mail.thexchangelab.com` as my namespace for URLs and I have a single Autodiscover record. Once done click **Next**.

In *Figure 4.10* you will need to enter the following information:

- Organization Name
- Department Name
- City
- State/Province
- Country/Region name

Once you have filled that in then click **Next**:

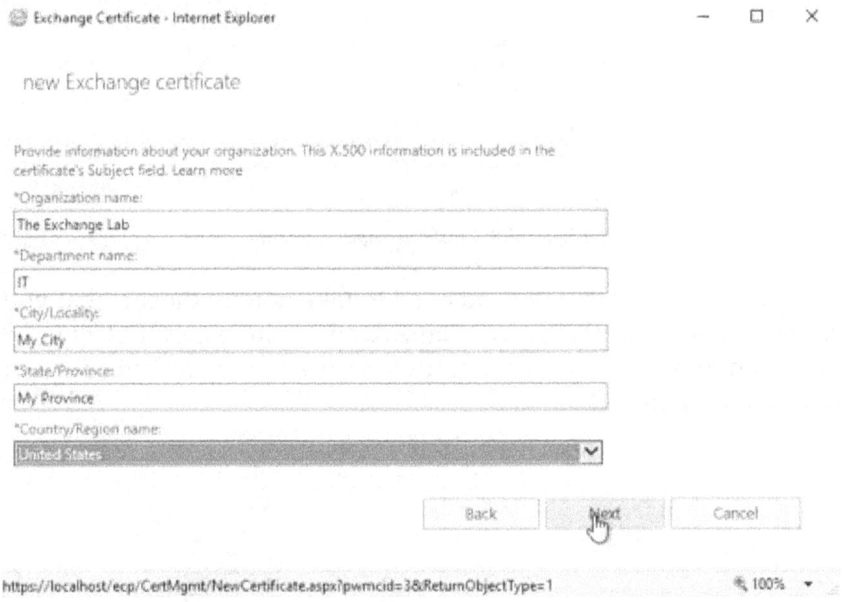

Figure 4.10: Provide information about your organization.

On the final screen shown below, enter the location where you want to save the file and then click **Finish**. In this example, I used \\localhost\C$\Mycert.REQ and then click **Finish**:

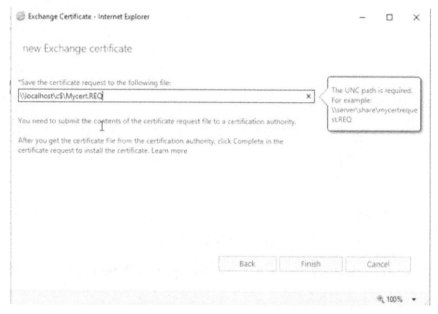

Figure 4.11: *Save the Certificate Request*

Once you have completed *Figure 4.11*, you will be taken back to the main certificates screen where you will now see your new certificate and it will be in a pending request state as shown in *Figure 4.12* below:

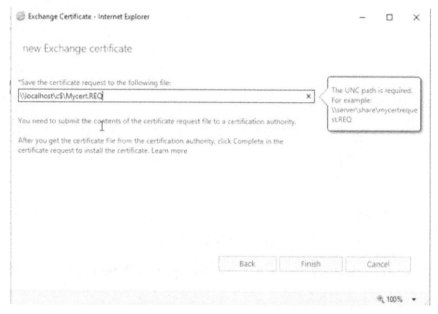

Figure 4.12: *Certificates Window*

Figure 4.13 below, is to show you that the file was saved:

Figure 4.13: *Windows Explorer*

You can access it by opening it with Notepad as Shown in *Figure 4.14* below:

Figure 4.14: *Certificate Request File*

Login to your provider of the choice website and create a new request with them and copy in the CSR information above. It will detect the names on the certificate that you chose in the wizard in Exchange. Once you have the file from your provider, click on the **Complete** button as shown in *Figure 4.15* as shown below:

Figure 4.15: *Complete Certificate Request*

A new window as shown in *Figure 4.16* below is where you will locate the file that you downloaded:

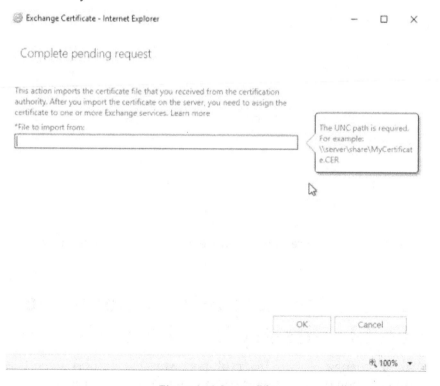

Figure 4.16: *Import File*

Once that is complete, you need to now assign services to your Certificate. In the **Exchange Admin Center (EAC)** select the certificate and then either double click it or click on the pencil to edit its properties.

A new window like *Figure 4.17* will show as per below, click on the **Services** tab and then select the services you want to assign to this certificate and then click **Save**:

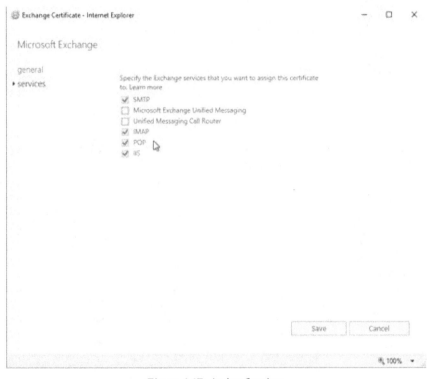

Figure 4.17: Assign Services.

Once the changes are completed, reboot your server for it to take effect.

Certificates – Exporting/Importing PFX file directly into IIS/Exchange

With Exchange, there are multiple ways to import/export a certificate. Some might prefer performing these steps from the EAC where others prefer using PowerShell and you can also import your SSL certificate into the IIS.

Let's take a step back, you just said Import/Export but I created a CSR? Yes, in IIS as an example, you can import your SSL certificate in PFX format and it will show up in Exchange. This you can do when you renew the same cert with your vendor.

You can also import/export an SSL certificate in the EAC.

Export

In the same place where you created your CSR, next to the refresh button you have 3 dots ..., this gives you 2 options, **Export Exchange Certificate** and **Import Exchange Certificate**. If you do not select any certificate, the Export option will be greyed out. If you have selected one and click **Export**, you should see a window like *Figure 4.18* below.

Here you can specify a path like \\localhost\c$\cert.PFX and provide a password for the certificate. Once done, you can click the **OK** button.

Figure 4.18: Export Exchange Certificate

Import

As this is a PFX file, you can import it into IIS as well directly, if you click Start and then click on **Administrative tools** a new window will open and here you can double click on **Internet Information Services (IIS) Manager.** It should look like *Figure 4.19* below:

Figure 4.19: *Import Certificate in IIS*

Click on the server name in question and the set of options double click server certificates. You will see above that you have an **Import** button. If you click this you will be presented with *Figure 4.20* below:

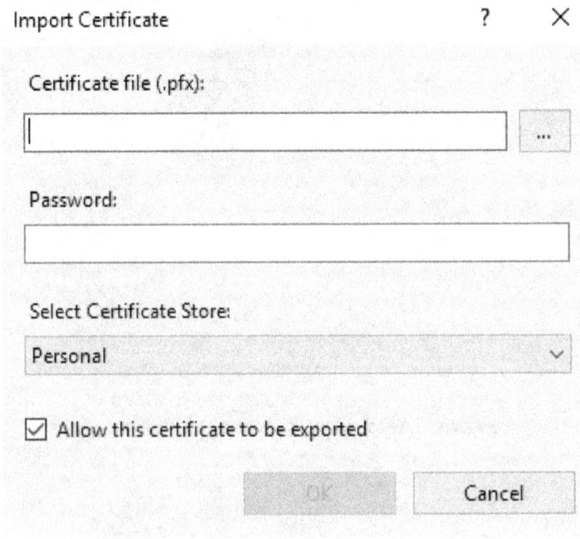

Import Certificate

Certificate file (.pfx):

Password:

Select Certificate Store:

Personal

☑ Allow this certificate to be exported

OK   Cancel

Figure 4.20: *Import Certificate*

Click the 3 dots button to the right and locate the file. Next, enter the password and then click **OK**. The certificate will now be imported and can be used to assign services in Exchange and update your bindings in IIS which we will cover in the next section.

Now in Exchange, you can do the same thing, just the window is different. In the same place where you Exported the Certificate in the EAC, click the **Import Exchange Certificate** button and you will be presented with *Figure 4.21* as shown below:

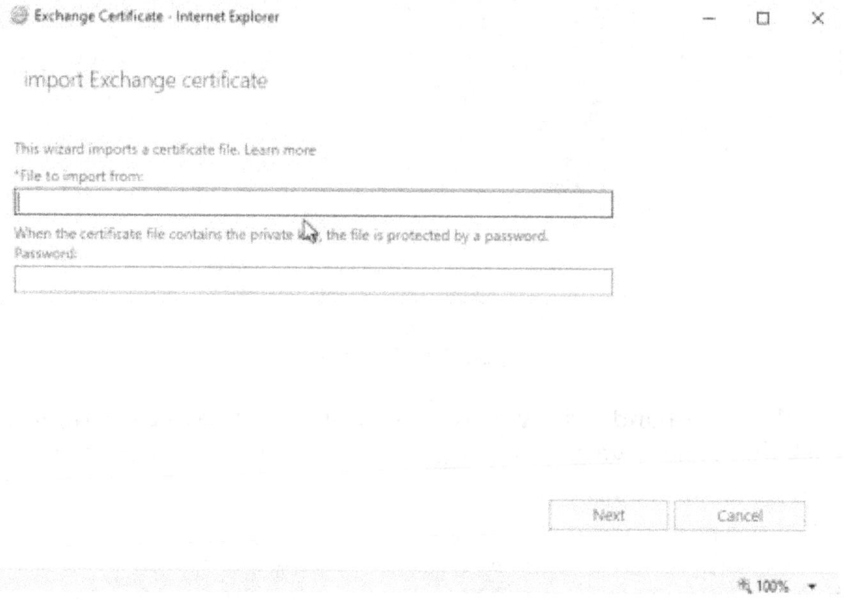

Figure 4.21: Specify Location to import SSL Certificate.

Here you will specify the location as you did with the **Export** and enter in the password and you will be able to assign services to the cert.

Certificates – Configuring IIS bindings to use your new SSL certificate

This is an easy section. The reason why you need to bind the default web site and exchange backend to your SSL certificate is so that clients using Outlook on the Web (OWA) and Outlook or email client of choice do not get certificate popups for the default exchange certificate.

To configure this, launch IIS as we did in the previous section, expand sites and click on **Default Web Site** as shown in *Figure 4.22* below:

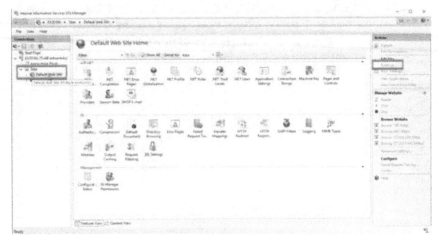

Figure 4.22: Bindings

On the right-hand side, you will see a link that says **Bindings**.... click this. A new window like *Figure 4.23* shown below will open:

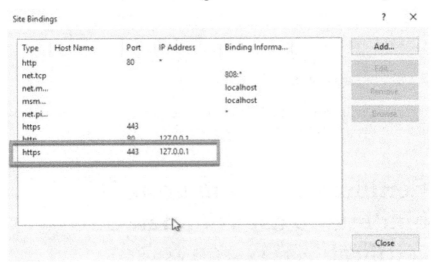

Figure 4.23: Configure Site Bindings

Now click on **https** as highlighted in *Figure 4.23* and select **Edit** on the right-hand side. A new window will open as shown in *Figure 4.24* below:

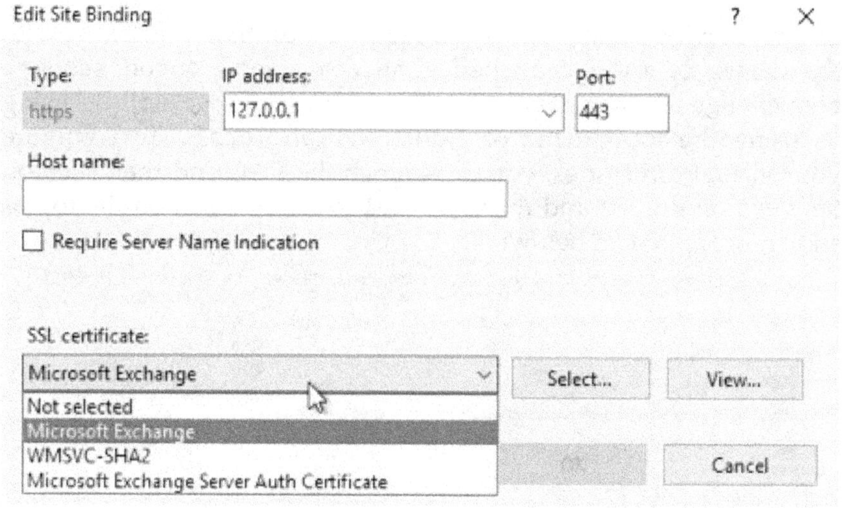

Figure 4.24: Select SSL Certificate

Click the dropdown list below the **SSL Certificate** and select the certificate you want to use. Once done click **OK** to go back to the previous window and then click **Close**. Perform the same step for the **Exchange Back End** site.

When you are finished, either launch an elevated Command Prompt and run IISReset or reboot your server for the changes to take effect.

Virtual directories – Configuring your virtual directories

In the last section of this chapter, we are going to look at configuring our virtual directories. The virtual directories to configure are as follows:

- Autodiscover
- ECP
- EWS
- MAPI
- Microsoft ActiveSync

- OAB
- OWA
- PowerShell

In the previous section, we configured our SSL certificate with the names of `mail.thexchangelab.com` and `Autodiscover.thexchangelab.com`. These are the namespaces we will be using vs using the local name of `EX2016A.tlab.local`. To configure your virtual directories, you can launch the EAC and then click on **Servers** on the left and then **Virtual Directories** on the top as shown in *Figure 4.25* below:

Figure 4.25: Virtual Directories

You can double click each one of them and configure the Internal/External URL, we will use one example of this and it will be the ECP as shown in *Figure 4.26* below:

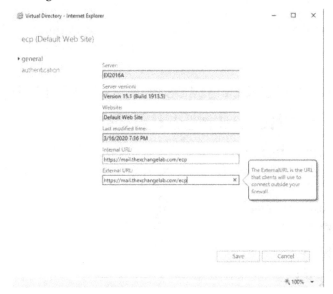

Figure 4.26: Edit Virtual Directory

To get to this window, simply double click on ECP (**Default Web Site**) and it will bring up the window above but with the internal server name in the **Internal URL** box and nothing in the **External URL** box. Click **Save** for the changes to be made. You can perform this now on EWS/MAPI/AS/OAB/OWA and PowerShell.

You will notice that I left out Autodiscover. This is because you cannot configure its URL on the EAC. It has to be done in PowerShell (EMS). You can configure all of these with PowerShell (EMS) instead of using the EAC. Here are the commands to use to update all of them:

```
Set-ClientAccessService -Identity Exchange-2016
-AutodiscoverServiceInternalUri https://mail.thexchangelab.
com/autodiscover/autodiscover.xml
```

```
Get-WebServicesVirtualDirectory -Server Exchange-2016 |
Set-WebServicesVirtualDirectory -InternalUrl https://mail.
thexchangelab.com/ews/exchange.asmx -ExternalURL https://
mail.thexchangelab.com/ews/exchange.asmx
```

```
Set-OWAVirtualDirectory -identity "Exchange-2016\
owa (Default Web Site)" -InternalURL https://mail.
thexchangelab.com/owa -ExternalURL https://mail.
thexchangelab.com/owa
```

```
Get-OABVirtualDirectory -Server Exchange-2016 | Set-
OABVirtualDirectory -InternalURL https://mail.
thexchangelab.com/OAB -ExternalURL https://mail.
thexchangelab.com/OAB
```

```
Get-ECPVirtualDirectory -Server Exchange-2016 | Set-
ECPVirtualDirectory -InternalURL https://mail.
thexchangelab.com/ECP -ExternalURL https://mail.
thexchangelab.com/ECP
```

```
Get-MAPIVirtualDirectory -Server Exchange-2016 | Set-
MAPIVirtualDirectory -InternalURL https://mail.
thexchangelab.com/MAPI -ExternalURL https://mail.
thexchangelab.com/MAPI -IISAuthenticationMethods
NTLM,Negotiate
```

```
Get-ActiveSyncVirtualDirectory -Server Exchange-2016 |
Set-ActiveSyncVirtualDirectory -InternalURL https://mail.
thexchangelab.com/Microsoft-Server-ActiveSync -ExternalURL
https://mail.thexchangelab.com/Microsoft-Server-ActiveSync
```

```
Set-OutlookAnywhere -identity "Exchange-2016\
RPC (Default Web Site)" -ExternalHostname mail.
```

```
thexchangelab.com -InternalHostname mail.thexchangelab.com
-InternalClientsRequireSSL $true -ExternalClientsRequireSsl
$true -ExternalClientAuthenticationMethod:NTLM
```

Once you have run all the commands above, reboot your server for the changes to take effect.

Conclusion

You have learnt in this chapter why you need to have a valid SSL certificate that Exchange 2016 needs to be configured with and why it is important that you update the binding in IIS to use your SSL certificate. You also have a good understanding of how to configure your virtual directories in Exchange 2016, not only using the Exchange Admin Center but using PowerShell and how simple it is to configure using PowerShell. Lastly, you should now be able to create your first certificate request (CSR) and submit this to a valid provider like GoDaddy or RapidSSL and then complete your request in Exchange and assign services to that certificate.

In the next chapter, you will have a good understanding of all the protocols that clients can use to connect to Exchange and how you can configure them using the graphical interface (GUI) which is the **Exchange Admin Center (EAC)** or the **Exchange Management Shell (EMS).**

Questions

1. **My internal CA certificate will work without an error on the internet?**

   Answer: Incorrect, you need a valid SSL certificate from a 3rd party so you do not receive errors when accessing your servers on the internet.

2. **I need to create a CSR and send the Request file to my SSL provider?**

   Answer: Yes your provider like Digicert or GoDaddy will ask you to provide a valid CSR to generate an SSL certificate.

3. **I can configure my Virtual Directories from the Exchange Admin and the Exchange Management Shell? (True or False)**

   Answer: True

CHAPTER 5

Client Connectivity

Email in most organizations now is the application that has to be up all the time. This means Exchange 2016 has to be highly available. Users today connect to Exchange 2016 using smartphones, tablets, notebooks, Apple devices, and any device that will have a mail client. Client connectivity has improved a lot with Microsoft introducing MAPI over HTTP and this is the preferred method of connectivity as it put less strain on the server. Users today are not office-bound and most of them work from home or in public places like coffee shops and they need to connect to Exchange 2016 using the protocol that the company provides to them.

In this chapter, we will be taking a look at the different ways clients can connect to Exchange. Here are the ways in which clients can connect to Exchange and we will explain each in detail. In chapter 4 we looked at configuring the URL's which will allow outside access to the protocols below.

Structure

- POP3
- IMAP4

- ActiveSync
- MAPI over HTTP
- Outlook Anywhere
- EWS (Used often by Mac Clients.)

Objectives

- Learn about the different protocols for connecting clients in Exchange 2016.
- Learn how to configure protocols like POP3 or IMAP4.
- Learn how to work in both the Exchange Admin Center and Exchange Management Shell to configure your protocols.

Let's dive into more detail.

POP3

POP has been around for a long time on Exchange and as the versions progressed the use of it has declined. There are still companies that will only use POP and won't make use of Outlook Anywhere or MAPI which we will talk about later on in this chapter. When you install an Exchange 2016 Server, POP3 is not enabled. If you want to enable it you need to change the following services to automatic:

- Microsoft Exchange POP3
- Microsoft Exchange POP3 Backend

So why do I have two services? They each service a function.

Microsoft Exchange POP3 provides service to clients. If this service is stopped clients cannot connect. *Microsoft Exchange POP3* Backend provides service to mailboxes. If this service is not started then mailboxes cannot be accessed.

If you like working in the GUI then launch the **Exchange Admin Center (EAC).** Click on **Servers** on the left-hand side and then servers on the right-hand side as shown in *Figure 5.1:*

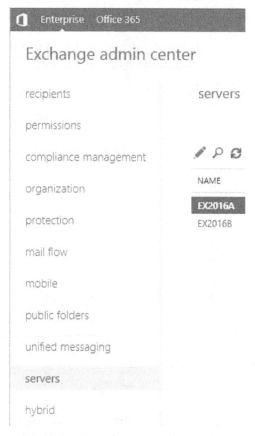

Figure 5.1: *Exchange Admin Center - Servers*

Now you can double click on a server that will be used for POP3 or click on a **Server** and then click on the **pencil** to edit the properties. On the new window click **POP3** as shown in *Figure 5.2:*

Figure 5.2: POP3 Settings

On this page you can configure your login method, Secure TLS is the default method. You can configure your banner. This is what people will see when they do telnet to your server on port **110** (unsecure) or **995** (secure). If you open the **Exchange Management Shell (EMS),** there are some additional settings you need to be aware of. As shown in *Figure 5.3* below, take note of the following:

- InternalConnectionSettings
- ExternalConnectionSettings

Figure 5.3: POP3 PowerShell settings

To get the information above, you need to run the following command:

```
Get-POPSettings - Server Server1 | fl
```

You need to configure these 2 items as when you configure a POP account and you connect to it externally, it will give you a certificate error because `tlab.local` is not valid. To configure this you can type in the following commands to update those fields:

```
Set-PopSettings -server Server1 -ExternalConnectionSettings
"pop3.thexchangelab.com:995:SSL","pop3.thexchangelab.
com:110:TLS" -X509CertificateName pop3.thexchangelab.com
```

```
Set-PopSettings -server Server1 -InternalConnectionSettings
"pop3. thexchangelab.com:995:SSL","pop3. thexchangelab.
com:110:TLS" -X509CertificateName pop3. thexchangelab.com
```

Finally, reboot your server or restart the POP3 services for the changes to take effect. As you can see, there are a few steps to complete the configuration of your services.

Remember you need to allow Port 110/995 on your firewall so that clients can connect

IMAP4

IMAP is just like POP3. It has been around for a long time. As with POP3, IMAP also has two services that need to be set to Automatic and started for IMAP to start working. They are as follows:

- Microsoft Exchange IMAP4
- Microsoft Exchange IMAP4 Backend.

Microsoft Exchange IMAP4 provides service to clients. If this service is stopped clients cannot connect. *Microsoft Exchange IMAP4 Backend* provides service to mailboxes. If this service is not started then mailboxes cannot be accessed.

Just like with POP3, you can access the IMAP4 settings by going to the Exchange Admin Center, clicking on **Servers** and then servers again and double click your **Server** and click on **IMAP4** as shown in *Figure 5.4* below:

Figure 5.4: IMAP4 Settings

On this page you can configure your login method, Secure TLS is the default method. You can configure your banner. This is what people will see when they do telnet to your server on port **143** (unsecure) or **993** (secure). If you open the **Exchange Management Shell (EMS),** there are some additional settings you need to be aware of. As shown in *Figure 5.5* below, take note of the following:

- InternalConnectionSettings
- ExternalConnectionSettings

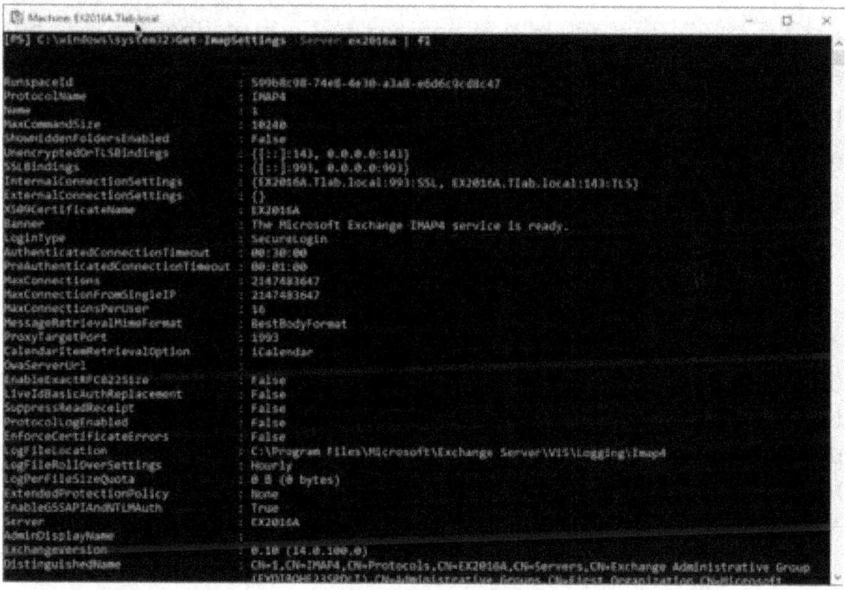

Figure 5.5: IMAP4 PowerShell Settings

You need to configure these 2 items as when you configure an IMAP4 account and you connect to it externally, it will give you a certificate error because `tlab.local` is not valid. To configure this you can type in the following commands to update those fields:

```
Set-ImapSettings -server Server1
-ExternalConnectionSettings "imap4.thexchangelab.
com:993:SSL","imap4.thexchangelab.com:143:TLS"
-X509CertificateName imap4.thexchangelab.com
```

```
Set-ImapSettings -server Server1
-InternalConnectionSettings "imap4. thexchangelab.
com:993:SSL","imap4. thexchangelab.com:143:TLS"
-X509CertificateName imap4. thexchangelab.com
```

Finally, reboot your server or restart the IMAP4 services for the changes to take effect. As you can see, there are a few steps to complete the configuration of your services.

ActiveSync (AS)

Exchange ActiveSync is a synchronization protocol to allow mobile phones to access an organizations' Exchange Server. In simple terms, it allows you to sync your company email to your phone. Unlike POP/IMAP, ActiveSync is enabled on Exchange 2016 by default. In previous chapter we configured the URL for Exchange 2016 ActiveSync so that when you connect to your mailbox it does not give you an error.

It is enabled by default for all users in Exchange. Many applications make use of ActiveSync. These include and are not limited to:

- Outlook for iOS and Android
- Apple Mail
- Android Mail client.
- Many other mail clients on all the stores.

Just because it is enabled does not mean you cannot control what is allowed on the mobile device. Some corporates provide company phones and these have to abide by rules defined in ActiveSync and this can include having a PIN enabled. You can also turn off access to ActiveSync on a mailbox. This can be done in the Exchange Admin Center or using PowerShell.

In the EAC, once you have logged in, click on **Recipients** and then mailboxes. Locate the mailbox you want to either double click it or click on the **pencil** to edit its properties. Now click on **Mailbox Features.** Under **Mobile** device, you can disable/enable the option for ActiveSync.

To do the same in PowerShell, you can run the following command:

```
Set-CASMailbox -Identity "User 1" -ActiveSyncEnabled $false
```

The command listed above is simple to use, some organizations use applications like Odin that control it from a central layer and that application runs the commands to enable or disable it.

MAPI over HTTP (MAPI)

MAPI over HTTP is the new way for clients to connect to an Exchange 2016 Server. In Exchange 2016 and higher versions, you can enable this across the organization or for individual mailboxes as well.

If you are running Exchange 2010 and you introduce Exchange 2016, MAPI over HTTP will be disabled org-wide by design. If you introduce a new domain with just Exchange 2016 then MAPI over HTTP will be enabled org-wide by design. Even if your Outlook client supports MAPI, if this is not enabled at an Exchange Server level it won't connect using this option.

When you perform an upgrade on an Exchange 2016 server, it will give you a warning in the setup that MAPI over HTTP is not enabled and is recommended.

Why would I want to use MAPI over HTTP when I can use the old RPC over HTTP?

There are a few benefits to this, namely:

- Providers faster reconnection times.
- Uses an HTTP based protocol.
- Device Hibernation.
- Changing from networks, being wired to wireless or cellular.

Will my Outlook clients work with this new method? Yes, but you need to be on the newer versions of Outlook. For example, Outlook 2013 with SP1 and higher versions of Outlook will be able to connect using MAPI over HTTP provided Exchange 2016 has it enabled. Can I leave MAPI over HTTP off in my environment? Yes, you can, Outlook clients will still connect using Outlook Anywhere which will cover later on in this chapter.

Configuration

In previous chapter we looked at configuring MAPI using the EAC and PowerShell. Even though you have configured your virtual directory, you need to also enable MAPI over HTTP in your environment. This can only be done using PowerShell and the `Set-OrganizationConfig` cmdlet. Here is the command:

```
Set-OrganizationConfig -MapiHttpEnabled $true
```

If you want to turn this off org-wide, then just replace the `$true` with `$false` in the command above. If you would like to configure MAPI over HTTP at the mailbox level then you can use PowerShell to enable it for a user, here is the command you can run:

Set-CasMailbox <User 1> -MapiHttpEnabled $true

In this section, you can see that Mapi over HTTP can be organization-wide or per user. Sometimes it's best to test per user so you do not impact the enter organization.

Outlook Anywhere (OA)

Outlook Anywhere has been the most preferred connection method before MAPI came round. On Exchange 2016 (also in Exchange 2013), Outlook Anywhere is enabled by default. In previous chapter we configured our URL for Outlook Anywhere using an SSL certificate. You can also configure your URLs and authentication methods from the EAC.

To access this from the EAC, login and then click on **Servers** on the Left-hand side and then servers on the right-hand side and then double click on a server or click the **pencil** to edit its properties. You will see a window similar to *Figure 5.6* below:

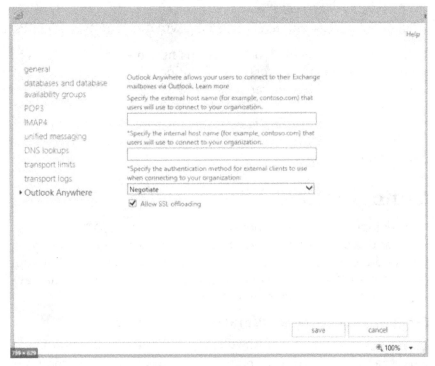

Figure 5.6: Outlook Anywhere.

Remember to ensure that the URLs you specify above in *Figure 5.6* match what you have on your SSL Certificate so you don't end up with user complaints about popups.

EWS (Exchange Web Services)

What is EWS and why do I need to configure it? Well EWS is there for you to be able to create your custom applications that can access mailbox stored data. To configure this is what was covered in previous chapter. You need to update your Web Services Virtual directory with the URL that can be accessed from the internet.

The URL when you do a test from Outlook should look like this:

https://mail.thexchangelab.com/EWS/Exchange.asmx

Now, this might look familiar? Yes because MAC clients use EWS to connect to Exchange. There are a number of EWS Operations in Exchange and is too exhaustive for this chapter to cover. Microsoft has a write-up about it here.

Conclusion

Now that you know end users can connect to Exchange 2016 using different protocols, you can go and set up your Exchange 2016 Server and configure your clients to use the method you want them to. You have learnt that MAPI over HTTP (the preferred protocol) is not enabled by default in an organization that is running coexistence with Exchange 2010 but is on by default with new forest and domain running Exchange 2016 only. Lastly, you have learnt that you can configure most of the protocols using the **Exchange Admin Center (EAC)** and also how to configure them using the **Exchange Management Shell (EMS).**

In the next chapter, you will learn about the different storage options that you can have in your environment or need to support in a customer environment. You will understand how to create a mailbox database using both methods which are with the Exchange Admin Center and the Exchange Management Shell and how to setup/

configure a **Database Availability Group (DAG)** in Exchange 2016. Lastly, you will know how to configure circular logging and also how to check your backups.

Questions

1. **What are the protocols you can configure clients to use to connect to your environment?**

    Answer: POP3, IMAP4, ActiveSync, Mapi, Outlook Anywhere.

2. **IMAP4 and POP3 Services are started automatically once you have installed your Server?**

    Answer: Incorrect, you need to both services for each protocol to automatic.

3. **Can you use the Exchange Admin Center to configure Outlook Anywhere?**

    Answer: Yes, you can by editing the properties of a server in the EAC.

4. **Exchange Web Services (EWS) can be used to create custom applications that can access mailbox data? (True or False)**

    Answer: True

5. **If you are running Exchange 2010 coexisting with Exchange 2016 Mapi over HTTP is enabled by default?**

    Answer: Incorrect, you need to manually enable it using PowerShell

CHAPTER 6

Databases and Database Availability Groups

Database availability groups also referred to as DAG's in short, provide you with the ability to set redundancy for your Exchange 2016 servers. This means that 2 or more servers form part of the DAG and the mailbox database stores are stored on these servers (copies which are either active or passive). If you have a 4 node DAG, for example, you could have 1 active store on each mailbox server and the other will be passive across the servers. Failover clustering is a component that is installed on a mailbox server that will be part of a DAG. It is important to note that this should not be the main section to manage your DAG as that is what Exchange 2016 does.

In this chapter, you will learn how to create a database availability group in your environment and how to manage it if you already have one. You will have an understanding of what is required for a DAG and why witness servers are important but also why they will not be used if you have a 3 node DAG as an example.

Structure

Here are the topics we will cover in this chapter:

- Storage – Mount points vs DAS (Direct Attached Storage), supported storage paths.
- Default Mailbox Database.
- Creating a mailbox database using PowerShell vs the GUI.
- Requirements for a Database Availability Group.
- Witness Servers and Directories.
- Creating your Database Availability Groups.
- Failover Clustering.
- Activation Preference and default move of Databases (Settings)

Circular logging, Backups, and what each one does.

Objectives

- Configure and explain the different types of storage
- Create a mailbox database
- Create a DAG
- Edit DAG properties to add members.
- Failover cluster and how it works
- Understand and manage Activation Preference on a DAG.
- Understand Circular logging and backups.

Storage

Storage has always been a big topic with Exchange. The reason I say this is because admins go and put Exchange with SQL or another storage-intensive application and they cannot understand why Exchange is slow. It is recommended that you put Exchange on its storage and not share it with any other application.

The first point we will talk about is Mount Points. This is a location on a SAN and is mapped to a folder on your server vs. giving it drive letters like in DAS which we will cover shortly. Let's take a step back. The storage admin will carve out LUN and volumes on the SAN for you to use. In the hypervisor whether its Hyper-V or VMWare, you will go and add disks to the server. Now depending on how many mailboxes you are hosting, you might have 4-5 stores. Most companies split the execs from the employees so each one is on a separate database.

The option of using Mount Points is expansion. Think of it as virtual storage. This chapter is not designed to talk about how to carve you LUN or Volume, it is merely explaining how to create mount points. The raid level on a SAN is pretty high so you can lose a number of disks because you might run into an issue. The next option is Direct Attached Storage (DAS). This means you have a physical server with an X amount of storage onboard.

You might purchase a Dell R730 or an HP Server that has 1TB of space as an example. You carve up space and raid for the OS and then the rest for data. Now you can configure your disks on Exchange and use drive letters. The only challenge with this is monitoring your space closely as this is a physical server with storage. Yes, you can extend most of them with a disk array but Admins generally only give Exchange X amount of space or the OS an amount and they cannot extend it so plan your storage well.

Default mailbox database

When you install Exchange 2016, you have a default mailbox database installed, this is called **Mailbox Database XXXXXXXXXX.** You can use this database to house your mailboxes but it is better to create your stores in Exchange and remove the default mailbox database. This is a personal choice. Some IT Admins prefer to keep things as they are when Exchange 2016 is installed or the company has defined how they want it structured.

Creating mailbox databases using PowerShell vs. using the EAC (Exchange Admin Center)

As mentioned above, when Exchange 2016 is installed, it creates a default mailbox database. Many admins create new mailbox databases and move the arbitration mailboxes off the default ones and then remove the default database. To create a mailbox database, you need to have a location for the database and log files. This will either be on a mount point as mentioned above or on DAS.

To create a mailbox database using PowerShell (EMS), you can run the following command:

```
New-MailboxDatabase -Server Server1 -Name "DAG01-STORE1"
-EdbFilePath C:\MountPoint\Store1 \DAG01-STORE1.edb
-LogFolderPath C:\MountPoint\Store1\Logs
```

As you can see, it is fairly easy to do. Now the biggest task is to wait for Active Directory replication. You might not see your new database yet or it will be in an unknown state before it goes into a healthy state. To create a mailbox database using the Exchange Admin Center can be done as follows:

Figure 6.1: Databases

Open the EAC and then login. Once logged in, click on servers and then databases as shown above in *Figure 6.1*. Click the + button to create a new **Mailbox Database** as shown in *Figure 6.2* below:

Figure 6.2: New Database

Enter the name of the database and the file path for the database and logs and click on the browse button to select a server to host the new database. You have the ability to **Mount the database** after creation by leaving the tick-box on or you can untick it and the database will be dismounted. Once you save this you will see your store as shown in *Figure 6.1:*

Requirements for creating a Database Availability Group (DAG)

Before you can go ahead and create a **Database Availability Group (DAG)** there are a few items to have in place. Your DAG name cannot be longer than 15 characters. If you are creating a DAG with an IP, then you need to add this to DNS so it can be resolved. If you plan on creating an IP-Less DAG then leave it blank.

The servers that will be part of the DAG need to have the same operating system. Yes, you cannot have a Windows 2012 R2 server and a Windows 2016 Server. They either need to both be Windows Server 2012 R2 or Windows Server 2016. The next thing to do is pre-stage the CNO. This means to create a computer object in Active Directory and add both servers as part of it (under the **Security** tab). Once you have done this, disable the computer account afterward. The reason is that when you create the DAG and it has added all Servers in, the object will be enabled.

Witness servers and directories.

There has been much improvement with Witness servers and directories in Exchange.

You can now optionally specify a witness server and a witness directory when creating your Database Availability Group. Don't I have to create a folder and share it and give the Exchange Trusted Subsystem rights? Yes, you can still do this. However, Microsoft now gives you the ability to leave those fields blank. This will in turn search for an Exchange Server that has the Client Access Services and will create a directory on that server, the default location for the directory is: (%SystemDrive%\DAGFileShareWitnesses\<DAG FQDN>)

On a Witness Server, you also need to add the **Exchange Trusted Subsystem** group to the **Administrators** group on the local Server. Take note this is not applicable to domain controllers.

Creating Database Availability Groups (DAG)

Before we dive into creating a DAG, let's start by answering what a DAG is. A DAG is a set of Exchange Mailbox servers (max 16) that provide automatic database failover. In simple terms, if you have a minimum of 2x servers in a DAG, they act as highly available to each other. For example, **store1** might be active on **Server1** and passive on **Server2,** **Server1** gets rebooted unexpectedly, or during a maintenance window to apply updates or upgrades the DAG is moved to the other side, it will continue to service clients while you carry out work on the backend.

> **You cannot mix servers in a DAG. Meaning, you cannot add an Exchange 2013 Server to an Exchange 2016 DAG, just like you cannot add an Exchange 2016 Server to an Exchange 2019 DAG.**

Back to the creation of the DAG. You can create a DAG using the Exchange Admin Center or with PowerShell. Let's look at the EAC for creating one first. Once you have logged in, click on Servers and then database availability groups as shown in *Figure 6.3* below:

Figure 6.3: Database Availability Group

You will notice a DAG is already present. Click the + button to add a new DAG. A new window will appear as shown in *Figure 6.4* below:

Figure 6.4: *New Database Availability Group*

Enter the name of the DAG. Enter in your Witness server and directory and then give it an IP address. If you want to go with an IP-Less DAG you can leave it blank and click **Save**. If you want to create a DAG using PowerShell, you can do that by running the following command:

```
New-DatabaseAvailabilityGroup -Name DAG01
-WitnessServer MBX01 -WitnessDirectory C:\DAG01
-DatabaseAvailabilityGroupIPAddresses 10.0.0.10
```

This is just an example, you can specify a lot more in the command if you want to. This is just providing the basics. Once you have your DAG created, there is one more step, adding your servers to the DAG.

In the Exchange Admin Center as shown in *Figure 6.3*, click on the DAG name and then click the second last icon next to the refresh button to **Manage the DAG** Membership as shown in *Figure 6.5* below:

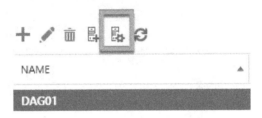

Figure 6.5: Modify DAG membership

This will bring up a new window as shown in *Figure 6.6* below:

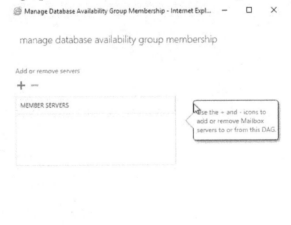

Figure 6.6: Manage Database Availability Group

Click on the + button to add your servers in. This will bring up another window (not shown here) for you to select your servers. Once you have selected your servers and they show up in the previous window, click **Save**. What this will do now is install Failover Clustering on all the Mailbox Servers you added to the list.

Reboot your servers afterward. Now that your DAG is in place, you can add mailbox database copies to the XXXX number of servers added to DAG. This can be done in the EAC by going back to the database and selecting a database and click the 3 ... button and selecting **Add database copy** as shown in *Figure 6.7* below:

Figure 6.7: *Databases view in the EAC.*

On the same screen, if you do not want Exchange 2016 to manage your networks you can click the icon next to membership on the left to add in a new DAG network.

Failover clustering

This is not a big topic but one you need to understand. Failover clustering is installed to make your servers highly available. This topic causing some confusion amongst new Exchange Admins. While you can manage a SQL cluster using Failover Clustering or Hyper-V servers, this is not the same with Exchange. The Failover clustering component is installed upon adding Exchange 2016 Mailbox database but should not be used to move your active/passive servers directly. You need to use Exchange for this.

There may come a time when you lose a DAG partner and have to do a clean-up and evict the dead node from the cluster but other than that all management should be done within Exchange 2016. Too often you see where they have gone and taken a server offline and cannot understand why Exchange starts to act up.

Activation preference and default move of databases

When Microsoft released Exchange 2016 CU2, a new option called PreferenceMoveFrequency. As shown in *Figure 6.8* below, this option is enabled by default and it is set to 1 hour. What this means is that if your Database is on the wrong activation preference it will be moved by Exchange. This is done by Active Manager. For some companies this might not seem like a viable option especially when dealing with a large number of users:

Figure 6.8: Exchange Management Shell to check DAG

You are able to disable this option, this can be done with a simple PowerShell command, here is the command, replace <DAGNAME> with the name of your DAG:

```
Set-DatabaseAvailabilityGroup -Identity <DAGName>
-PreferenceMoveFrequency ([System.Threading.
Timeout]::InfiniteTimeSpan)
```

Once the command has completed, you need to restart the Microsoft Exchange Replication Service.

Circular logging vs. Backups and the difference

In this section, we will talk about both technologies so you understand what each one does.

Circular logging

Microsoft has an option that you can enable circular logging on a Database. Some make the mistake of thinking that this is a backup because logs are flushed. The latter is true, it does flush the logs but does not do your backups. You would generally enable circular logging when you have 4 or more copies of an Exchange 2016 database in your environment. To enable circular logging is pretty straight forward.

Log into the **Exchange Admin Center (EAC),** click on Servers on the left-hand side and then click on **Databases** in the middle section. Double click on a database to view its properties or click the **pencil** icon to do the same and then click on the **Maintenance** tab in the new window as shown in *Figure 6.9* below:

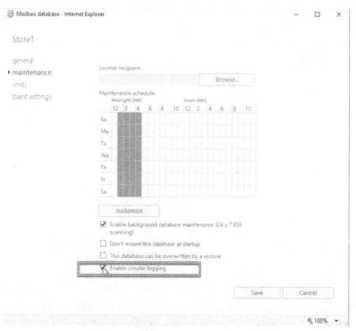

Figure 6.9: Enable Circular logging

Circular logging has been used when log files go missing, this can be from Anti-Virus exclusions not being set and it deletes files and after a reboot or during maintenance the Databases don't want to mount because of inconsistency, you can enable **Circular Logging** which will flush all the logs and will allow you to get them back online, however you will need to turn it off again and run a full backup.

Backups

The exchange needs to be backed up, especially if you running a single server with no DAG or 2/3 servers in a DAG. The backup truncates the log file and on the database, in Exchange, it flags when the last backup was done as shown in *Figure 6.10* below:

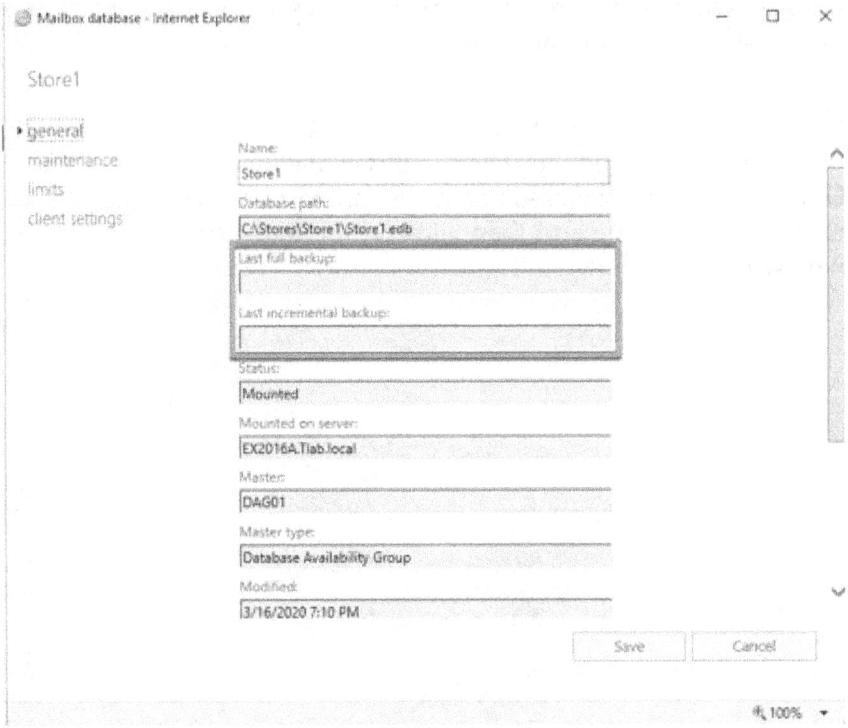

Figure 6.10: Check the last full backup of a Mailbox Database.

Now you get some backup software that is DAG aware and others not. What this means is that the backup software knows where the active/passive databases are. If it isn't DAG aware, you need to point the backup to a specific server. Doing Full server backup will not truncate the log files.

**Please take note that snapshotting Exchange Servers is not supported by Microsoft. If you are doing snapshots, please go back to the vendor and advise them they need to provide you with a solution that backs up Exchange and it's log files.

When restoring backups, its best to create a restore database and then do a recovery there and not overwrite the existing database. You will notice in *Figure 6.9* there is an option to allow it.

Conclusion

By now you should know what a database availability group is and how to either set one up or configure an existing one. You have also been shown how to set the activation preference to null as the default value for Exchange 2016 is 1 hour when Exchange 2016 will check if the mailbox database stores are on the correct servers. You learnt how you can check if your database has been backed up by logging into the **Exchange Admin Center (EAC)** and checking the properties. You now know that you cannot enable circular logging and have backups running as it will put your database into an inconsistent state

In the next chapter, you will learn what public folders are if you are new to Exchange 2016 and how you can manage your public folders directly from the Exchange Admin Center in Exchange 2016 compared to opening a separate console as you did in Exchange 2010. You will also learn how to create a public folder mailbox and folders and lastly how to perform a migration of public folders from Exchange 2010 to Exchange 2016.

Questions

1. **I can use the default database that is created when you install Exchange?**

   Answer: Yes you can, you can also remove it and create new stores.

2. **Name two ways you can create a mailbox database?**

   Answer: You can create a mailbox database using the Exchange Admin Center or the Exchange Management Shell.

3. **A database availability group (DAG) can be created with an IP address or without an IP address? (True or False)**

   Answer: True, you are not forced to use an IP when creating a DAG. Both options are True.

4. What is the default value of the `PreferenceMoveFrequency` (Activation Preference) available on a DAG in Exchange 2016?

   Answer: The default value is 1 hour.

5. You can view the last full backup of a mailbox database from the properties of the database in the EAC? (True or False)

   Answer: True

CHAPTER 7
Public Folders

Public folders are a great way to share information within an organization. You can create folders and subfolders and give certain users access to those like Finance and Marketing, etc. You can also use Public folders as an archiving method and you can mail-enable public folders.

Public folders have been improved from legacy versions where you had an extra database you needed to manage but could not make it redundant. This whole architecture changed starting in Exchange 2013 where Public Folders now is just a mailbox and is highly available if you have a DAG configured. You will learn how to access Public folders using the Exchange Admin Center and how to create the public folder mailboxes and your folder structure in the environment.

Let's first answer a question. What are public folders? It is a feature in Microsoft Exchange to share information within an organization. Access to public folders is controlled at an Admin level, so you can create a folder called Marketing as an Example and add only that department access. You can also have a general folder where everyone can share information like classifieds or job openings within the company.

Structure

What will be covered in this chapter?

- Public Folders in Exchange 2016 vs. 2013 and 2010
- High Availability for Public Folders
- Migration of Public folders

Objectives

- Understand how public folders have evolved.
- Explanation of public folders and high availability.
- Migrations.

Let's take a walk through each of the versions of Exchange and explain how public folders have evolved.

Public folders in Exchange 2010, Exchange 2013 and Exchange 2016

In Exchange 2010, you could create a Public Folder Database however this could only be added to a single server. To manage Public Folders you would need to login to the **Exchange Management Console (EMC)** and click on **Toolbox** and then to the right double click on **Public Folder Management Console** as shown in *Figure 7.1* below:

Figure 7.1: Public folder management

Once you have that window open then you could connect to the server that has public folders and create your folder structure. In the Exchange Security Groups in Active Directory, you have a Public Folder Management Group where you can add people who will manage the public folders.

Exchange 2013/2016

I have grouped these two versions as they perform the same function when it comes to Public Folders. In Exchange 2013, the big change was that Public Folders was no longer a database but a mailbox. This meant you didn't have to manage an extra store. The same applies to Exchange 2016, it is now a mailbox. It is very simple to create a Public Folder Mailbox and you can do this from the EAC.

In *Figure 7.2* below, once logged into the EAC, click on **Public Folders** on the left and the public folder mailboxes on the right:

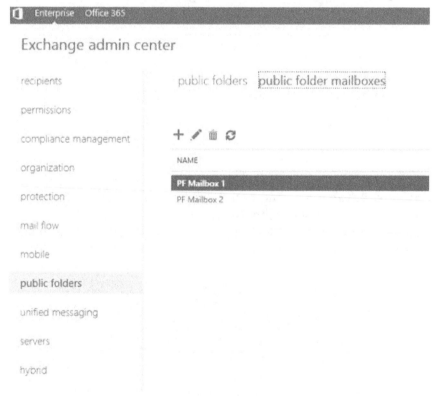

Figure 7.2: Public Folder Mailboxes

You can now click on the + plus button to create a new mailbox, once you have clicked the + button a new window will show as in *Figure 7.3* below:

Figure 7.3: *Create a new public folder mailbox*

All you need to do is give it a name and place it in an OU and on a **Mailbox Database**. Going back to *Figure 7.2*, you can click **Public Folders** next to Public Folder Mailboxes and you can click the + plus button to add a new folder. Once you have added a folder, it will appear in the main window as shown in *Figure 7.4* below:

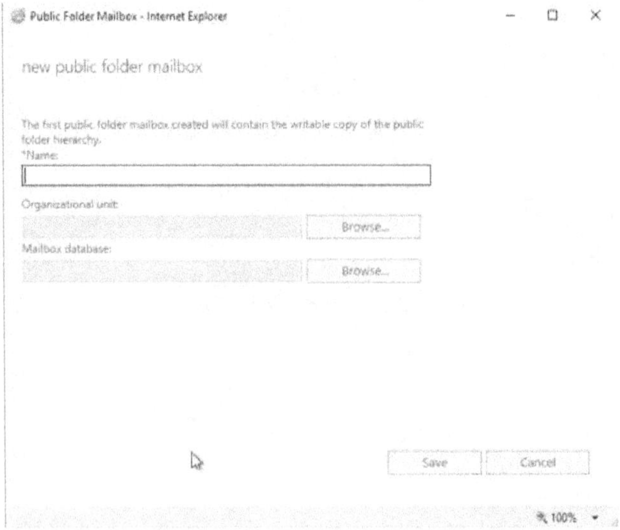

Figure 7.4: *New Public folder mailbox*

On the right-hand side, you can click **Manage** to adjust the folder permissions. Here you can add the users that need access or take away access. This is the simplicity of Public Folders now in Exchange 2016.

High availability for Public Folders

As you have seen, in Exchange 2010 a public folder database was added to a single server. You could not add it to a DAG and it was not highly available. This means it was a single point of failure and backups are critical. However in Exchange 2013 and 2016, as this is now a mailbox, it is part of the Mailbox Database and if this database is part of a DAG, it will be highly available.

Migration of Public folders

This is the heart of Public folders! Migrations! If you want to migrate your public folders from a legacy version to Exchange, you can do so only if you are on a certain SP (Service Pack – Exchange 2010) and Rollup (Exchange 2010) and for the newer versions CU (Cumulative Update). You can navigate to the link below for more information on what versions are supported:

https://docs.microsoft.com/en-us/exchange/collaboration/public-folders/faq?view=exchserver-2016

To migrate Public Folders from Exchange 2010 to Exchange 2016, there are some scripts that need to be downloaded and need to be executed. We are not going to cover this in great detail as it is beyond the scope of this book. To download the scripts and perform the migration, head over to the Microsoft link below:

https://docs.microsoft.com/en-us/exchange/collaboration/public-folders/batch-migration-from-previous-versions?view=exchserver-2016

Conclusion

As an IT Admin or specialist that manages Exchange, you now have a clear understanding of how you can manage public folders in your environment and also how to perform migrations of public folders from Exchange 2010 to Exchange 2016. You learnt that you can manage public folders from within the **Exchange Admin Center**

(EAC) instead of opening the public folder management console which was in Exchange 2010. You also learnt how to create a new Public folder Mailbox as well as creating the folders and granting access to users in Exchange 2016.

In the next chapter, you will learn how to configure unified messaging in your environment and customer environments and how you can access the option from within the Exchange Admin Center to configure your gateway. Finally, we share the links that list what is required to perform a Migration from Exchange 2010/2013 Unified Messaging to Exchange 2016 unified Messaging.

Questions

1. **Exchange 2016 has the option to create a public folder database?**

    Answer: Incorrect, the public folder database option was removed and a public folder mailbox now exists in Exchange 2016.

2. **A public folder mailbox is highly available now in Exchange 2016? (True or False)**

    Answer: True

CHAPTER 8
Unified Messaging

Unified messaging was introduced in legacy versions of Exchange and this gave you the ability to integrate your Exchange servers with Lync 2010 when it came out as well Lync 2013 and then you had Skype for Business 2016 which Exchange 2013/2016 could connect to. This gave the user the ability to see the presence in Outlook. A user could see if someone was in a meeting or away from their desk. It also gave you the ability to listen to voice mail and make calls directly from your outlook client.

Structure

What we will cover in this chapter is as follows:

- Unified Messaging in Exchange 2016
- Migration plan for transferring UM to Exchange 2016 from Exchange 2013 or legacy versions of Exchange.

Objectives

- Compare unified messaging to legacy versions of Exchange.
- Plan your migration of UM to Exchange 2016.

Unified Messaging in Exchange 2016

What is unified messaging? It enables users to voice mail and other features. If you are using Skype for Business Server, you can integrate it with Exchange 2016 and you will have what is known as the presence in Outlook. This shows when you are in a meeting, away from your desk and available, etc. Users have the ability to listen to voice messages from there inbox.

There are new features available in Exchange 2016 compared to Exchange 2010 and 2013. What features are available for end-users?

- Play voice messages on your mobile phone.
- Access to Exchange Information
- Call answering
- Call answering rules
- Voice mail form
- User configuration

These are only but a few, you can head over to the link below for additional information:

https://docs.microsoft.com/en-us/exchange/unified-messaging-exchange-2013-help

It is straight forward to configure Unified Messaging dial plans and IP gateways and you can do this from the **Exchange Admin Center (EAC)** as shown in *Figure 8.1* below:

Figure 8.1: UM IP Gateways

UM, IP Gateways needs to be configured for the UM server so it can communicate with it. This can be an object in Active Directory that has an IP address of the physical device in the environment.

Migration plan for transferring UM to Exchange 2016 from Exchange 2013 or legacy versions of Exchange

To perform a migration might take you a little while as there are a few steps you have to go through and this includes running scripts, moving system mailboxes, etc. Here are the steps:

1. Download and install the required UM Language packs.
2. Move your system mailboxes used for UM to Exchange 2016.
3. Microsoft list this as optional to export your dial plans and auto attendant, etc.
4. Export and Import Certificates.
5. Configure the UM startup mode on all 2016 servers.
6. Create or configure existing UM Dial plans.
7. Create or configure existing UM IP gateways.
8. Create a UM hunt group.
9. Create or configure UM Auto attendants.
10. Create or configure UM Mailbox Policies.
11. Move existing UM-enabled mailboxes to Exchange 2016.
12. Enable new users for UM or configure existing settings.
13. Configure your VOIP gateways etc. to point to the Exchange 2016 servers.
14. Disable call answering on Exchange 2010 UM server.
15. Remove Exchange 2010 UM Server from a Dial Plan.

As you can see, the list is quite extensive and you can follow each section in the link below:

https://docs.microsoft.com/en-us/exchange/upgrade-exchange-2010-um-to-exchange-2013-um-exchange-2013-help

The migration might seem like something that will take longer but it is an easy migration to do. Follow the steps and do not skip any. Most vendors have quite extensive knowledge of this as their equipment needs to work with exchange and Lync/Skype for business.

Conclusion

Now that you have a better understanding of how unified messaging works and can be configured in Exchange 2016, performing migrations of unified messaging from other versions of Exchange should not be a difficult task. Unified Messaging might seem like a complicated portion of Exchange 2016 to configure but it is straight forward.

In the next chapter, you will have a good understanding of how to perform mailbox moves using Migration batches as well as using PowerShell `cmdlets` to perform mailbox moves and also how to configure mailboxes that won't move due to corrupted items. Lastly, you will learn where to configure the MRS settings to increase the number of moves at a time.

CHAPTER 9

Migrations

When you introduce a new version of Exchange in your environment, to make use of all the new features and versions of Outlook you need to perform mailbox moves. This means moving from *Server A (Legacy Exchange)* to *Server B (Exchange 2016)*. Migrations can also be done if you need to move mailboxes from one database to another database as you want to get rid of white space or you want to balance out mailbox databases and for example, put Execs on their store.

Migration batches make it easy for you to do migrations. You can specify an excel spreadsheet to import and let Exchange do the migration. Mailbox moves can also be performed, also in bulk or individually.

Structure

In the chapter, we will go through each of the options below to understand how they work and also configure MRS to speed up migrations from Exchange 2010 to Exchange 2016.

- Migration batches in Exchange 2016

- Mailbox moves in Exchange 2016
- Migration from Exchange 2010 to 2016.
- Corruption in the mailbox and how it affects moves.
- Configuration of MRS to speed up mailbox moves.

Objectives

- Understand how migration batches work.
- Perform mailbox moves in Exchange 2016
- Understand corruption in mailboxes.
- Configure the legacy and current servers to speed up mailbox moves.

Migration batches in Exchange 2016

Migration batch put simply is moving a single user or multiple users that have a batch name. For example, you might move all Execs and call the migration Exec migration or Sales Migration or IT Migration. To start a migration batch, you need to login to the **Exchange Admin Center (EAC)**. Once you have logged in, click on **Recipients** and then **Migration** as shown in *Figure 9.1* below.

Exchange Admin Center

Below is a snippet of the Exchange Admin Center and we are focusing on the **Migrations** Tab under **Recipients**:

Figure 9.1: Migration tab in the EAC

As you can see, batch history is saved, in the above snippet, you will see a test batch I created. To start a new batch, simply click the arrow next to the + plus button and select **Move to a different database** as shown in *Figure 9.2*:

Figure 9.2: Create a new migration batch.

A new window will appear. The default option is **Select the users that you want to move** as shown in *Figure 9.3*. You also have the option to specify a CSV file which can contain multiple users, either option works:

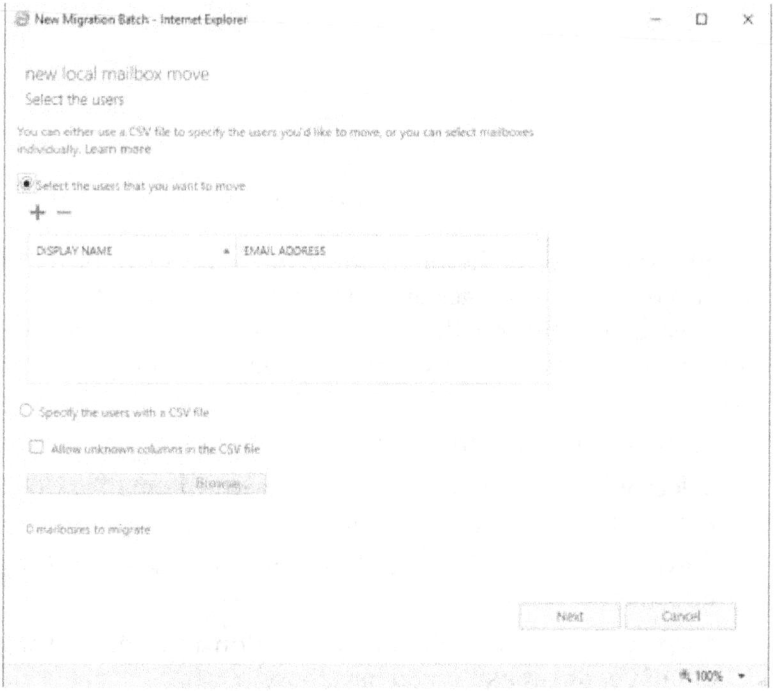

Figure 9.3: New Migration Batch window.

Click the + plus button, a new window will show with all users that have mailboxes as shown in *Figure 9.4* below:

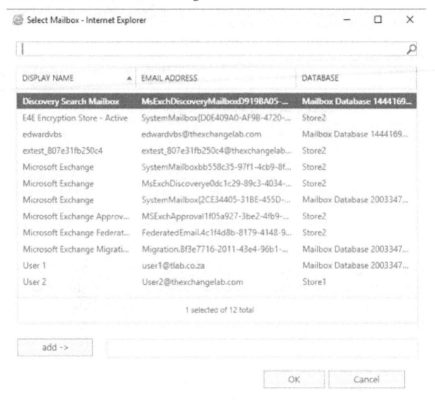

Figure 9.4: Select mailboxes to move.

Once you have selected the users, click the **add -> ** button at the bottom and then **OK**. Now back at the main **Migration Batch** screen, it will show the list of users that will be moved. Now click **Next**. On the next page (*Figure 9.5*) shown below, you can now perform the following:

1. Provide a **Migration Batch Name.**

2. Select whether you want to only move the mailbox or the archive mailbox if you have any.

3. Next, you will click the browse button to select a **Target database.**

4. Next, you will click the browse button to select a **Target archive database** if you have one.

5. Lastly, specify a **Bad item limit** and then click **Next**

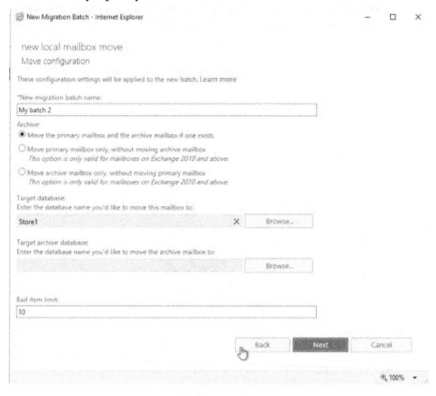

Figure 9.5: *Select the options for this mailbox migration batch.*

On the final page, you will select a recipient who will get a report. Once selected then make your selection on how you want the batch to start and complete as shown in *Figure 9.6*:

Figure 9.6: *Select the options for the migration batch.*

Once you have clicked **new** you will be taken to the main migration window as shown in *Figure 9.1* above. If you click on **View Details** on the right, you can see what is happening with the batch as shown in *Figure 9.7* below:

Figure 9.7: *View details of the current batch.*

You don't need to be in the migration tab to do moves. From the recipient's tab, you can select a mailbox and on the right-hand side you can click the link **To another database** and the new batch window will start.

PowerShell

The same can be achieved using PowerShell. Launch the **Exchange Management Shell (EMS)** and type in the following command to create a migration batch:

```
Get-Mailbox -Database "Store1" | New-MoveRequest -BatchName
"Store 01 to Store 02" -TargetDatabase "Store2" -Priority
High -BadItemLimit 50 -AcceptLargeDataLoss
```

Now below is a simple move request, don't confuse them.

```
New-MoveRequest -Identity user3@thexchangelab.com
-PrimaryOnly -TargetDatabase "Store2" -BadItemLimit 10
```

In *Figure 9.8* you can see the command in action:

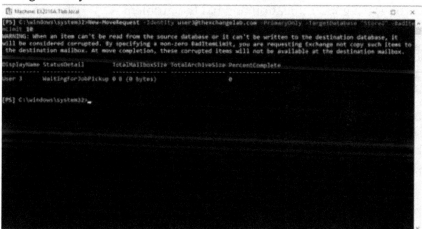

Figure 9.8: *Create a new mailbox moves request in the EAC.*

You can also select a database and move it using PowerShell vs. doing batches at a time, just take note that you need space to do this. So how do I check my batch moves? It is simple actually, you can run the following command in your EMS window.

You can use a broad command like Get-MoveRequest -BatchName * and this will list all migration batches:

```
Get-MoveRequest -BatchName "My Batch 2"| Format-List
DisplayName, Alias, Status, *database*
```

You can see above how easy it is to perform mailbox moves with PowerShell. Remember that the EAC does PowerShell commands in the background.

Mailbox Moves in Exchange 2016

Mailbox moves can be done from the **Exchange Management Shell (EMS)** on the fly, meaning at any time. *Figure 9.8* showed you a local move. To perform a local move, you can click on the recipient in the EAC and select the option to move to another database or you can use PowerShell. With PowerShell, you can also import a CSV file. You need to take note of the requirements for local moves in the CSV file. You can refer to the link here for a detailed description:

https://docs.microsoft.com/en-gb/exchange/csv-files-for-mailbox-migration-exchange-2013-help

Mailbox moves in Exchange 2016 are not complicated to start or to figure out why they have failed or why the moves have stalled. It gives you a good indication of what the problem is.

Migration from Exchange 2010 to 2016.

In *Chapter 1: Introduction to Exchange 2016* we spoke about coexistence so we not going to speak too much about that. If we fast forward a bit, you have your Exchange 2016 server installed and configured. All post configurations are complete and you either using a single namespace or disjointed namespace.

Now comes the task for moving mailboxes. You can pick your poison, it can either be batches or using the new-moverequest cmdlet. If you are using a 3rd party layer like Odin on top of Exchange, you can select the mailboxes at will and let them move.

Let's say you have a manager and the manager has delegate access to his/her mailbox, you need to move them together as there has will be a disconnect. Depending on the size of the mailboxes the moves will take time.

Corruption in the mailbox and how it affects moves

Corruption in mailboxes happens. You would have noticed in *Figure 9.5* we did not change the default **Bad item limit** of **10**. What this means is that it will allow the move to happen up to 10 bad items, after that the move will fail. As per Microsoft, you should not go higher than 50 in the EAC. If you need to increase the value then you need to use the **Exchange Management Shell (EMS)** to set it and also include the AcceptLargeDataLoss switch with the BadItemLimit.

Let's say you have 20 mailboxes moving and they all fail, you can run the following command to set the limits:

```
Get-MoveRequest | Set-MoveRequest -BadItemLimit 100
-AcceptLargeDataLoss
```

Once it completes, you can resume all the mailbox moves. To do this you can run the following command:

```
Get-MoveRequest | Resume-MoveRequest
```

You can also only perform the command for only 1 user, you can use the following command:

```
Get-MoveRequest -Identity "User 3" | Set-MoveRequest
-BadItemLimit 51 -AcceptLargeDataLoss
```

Figure 9.9 shows an example of this:

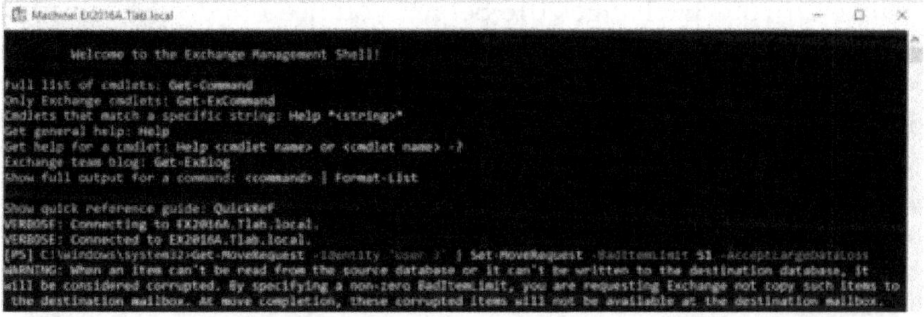

Figure 9.9: *Check your move requests in the EMS.*

If a mailbox keeps failing do not keep increasing the limit, either run a repair on the mailbox or export everything to PST and re-create the mailbox (worst case).

Configuration of MRS to speed up mailbox moves

When you perform mailbox moves, Exchange 2010 (*Source*) and Exchange 2016 (*Destination*) do have limits enabled for the number of mailboxes that can be moved at a given time. This ensures that you don't exhaust the resources on the server. There are a couple of things you can check prior to doing migrations to ensure you do not have a network bottleneck:

- Ensure that your Anti-Virus exclusions are in place.

- You can copy a file from source to destination to see how long it takes. As an example, we copied a 7 GB file and it copied at about 350mb/s which was pretty quick.

- If you have backups running, you need to ensure that backups are not running during the migration process.

- Start with a small set of users and grow it. It does not help you throw resources at a server.

If you want to monitor the migrations, you can open `PerfMon` and monitor the CPU, Memory, and Storage. The next option is to modify the `MSExchangeMailboxReplication.exe.config` file located in `C:\Program Files\Microsoft\Exchange Server\V15\Bin`

Make a backup first before you modify this file and launch Notepad elevated to ensure you can save changes to the file. If you make a change on your Exchange 2016 Server, you need to do the same on your Exchange 2010 Server. In *Figure 9.10* below you can modify the entries to increase the moves. Just be aware that you might run into other issues:

Figure 9.10: *MRS Configuration section.*

These issues can include 1 of the following:

- `Stalleduetotarget_dataguaranteewait`
- `Stalleduetotarget_mdbreplication`
- `Stalleduetohigherpriorityjobs`
- `StalleduetoCI`
- `Stalledtotarget_disklatency`
- `Relinquishedwlmstall`

Generally, after the time limits configured in the file above, the moves will resume and carry on.

Conclusion

Now you have an understanding of how to perform mailbox migrations in your environment or within your customers' environment either using batches or using move request `cmdlets`. You also now know how to set limits for mailboxes that have corrupted items in them. By setting the bad item limit you are telling Exchange to skip over that item it encounters that is corrupt. The larger the limit set the more items it will skip once the migration happens. Lastly, you have the ability to increase your mailbox moves from Legacy to Exchange 2016 by modifying the MRS settings defined for mailbox moves.

In the next chapter, we will take a look at how to work with the Exchange Management Shell and how you can configure your entire organization using just PowerShell and also how to use the Exchange Admin Center which is now web-based and you no longer need to launch a management console.

Questions

1. **You can use a migration batch to migrate 1 user or multiple users with a CSV. (True or False)**

   Answer: True, migration batches do not need to be groups of users, you can move 1 user to test migrations.

2. **How can you view the progress of your migration batches?**

   Answer: Using PowerShell or the Exchange Admin Center.

3. I have a mailbox that keeps failing due to corrupt items, I can use the set-moverequest cmdlet with the -baditemlimit option to skip corrupt items? (True or False)

    Answer: True

4. If you specify a bad item limit of 51, what switch do you need to include in your command?

    Answer: You need to include the `-AcceptLargeDataLoss` option.

5. In the MRS configuration file, I am able to increase the limits to allow more mailboxes to move at a time? (True or False)

    Answer: True, Microsoft provides default values and these can be changed.

CHAPTER 10

Exchange Management Shell vs. EAC

The Exchange Management Shell is the main place you will be configuring and maintaining your Exchange 2016 environment. If you are an organization admin, you have full control over everything that can be set in the Management Shell and you also have the ability to create new role groups and assign members to each while you teach them. The Exchange Admin Center is web-based now compared to the old Exchange Management Console. The Exchange Admin Center is limited to what you can set in Exchange but for anyone new and not familiar with PowerShell it is a great way to start learning how to use it.

In this chapter, we will show you the Exchange Admin Center and how you can view the commands it runs in the background and how to configure WinRM to allow remote connections. We will also take a look at the older commands and some of the new ones.

Structure

In this chapter we will be working with the following options:

- Configuring WinRM for the **Exchange Management Shell (EMS)**

- Using the Exchange Management Shell, new commands vs. old commands
- Using the Exchange Admin Center
- Viewing the commands that run in the background when the links in the EAC are clicked

Objectives

- Understand WinRM and how to configure it
- Working in the Exchange Admin Center
- Viewing commands run from the Exchange Admin center

WinRM

In Exchange, if you run a command from Server A to get the server version as an example, you might end up with an error saying that you need to run winrm quick config to allow remote connections. To do this you can run the following command from an elevated command prompt or elevated PowerShell window:

Winrm qc or

Winrm quickconfig

Figure 10.1 has an example of this command:

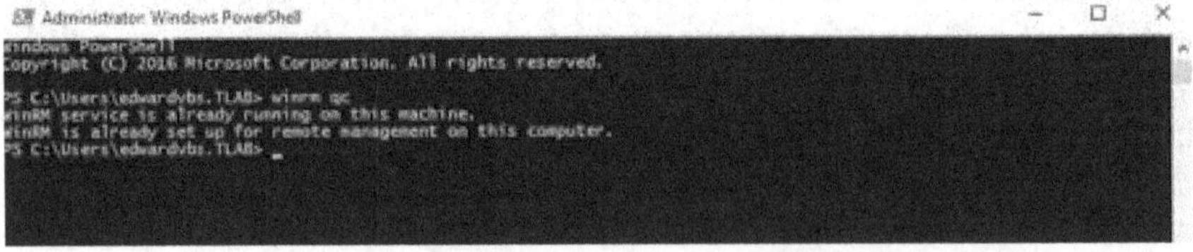

Figure 10.1: *Configure WinRM.*

If it has not been configured, you will be prompted with another question to create a listener on HTTP://*

Now you can lock this down to specific IP's but that is out of the scope of this book. Once you have completed the above, it should start accepting requests and you should be able to get the information needed.

Using the Exchange Management Shell, new commands vs. old commands.

As Exchange has evolved, so has the commands. If we go back to Exchange 2010 you had 5 roles, with Exchange 2016 you only have 2 and so the commands will update. If we take a simple command like `Get-TransportServer`, in Exchange 2010 you would not be given any warning.

However, in Exchange 2016 and higher, you will receive a nice 3 liner warning to advise you to use a new command going forward. In *Figure 10.2* below, you will notice that we ran `Get-TransportServer` and even though it came back with the correct information, it advised us to use the cmdlet `Get-TransportService instead`. *Figure 10.2* has an example below of the old commands:

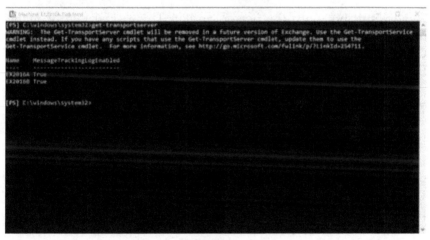

Figure 10.2: *Viewing the old commands in the EMS*

Now if we run the new cmdlet, we do not receive any warning as shown in *Figure 10.3* below:

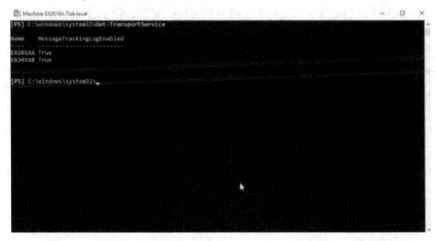

Figure 10.3: Viewing the new commands in the EMS.

Same result but with the newer cmdlet. This is just one of many new ones. Another example of this is using the cmdlet `Get-ClientAccessServer` which you would use in Exchange 2010 but in Exchange 2016 you would use `Get-ClientAccessService`.

Using the Exchange Admin Center.

If we quickly take a step back to Exchange 2010, you would use the **Exchange Management Console (EMC)** to perform a certain set of functions. In Exchange 2016 this is called the **Exchange Admin Center (EAC)** as we have referred to many times in this book. The EAC is a Web-based management console. It replaced the EMC that we had in Exchange 2010.

Like EMC, the EAC is limited in what it can do. As mentioned in earlier chapters, most companies are disabling access to the EAC due to the surface attack on Exchange, not only 2016, Exchange 2013 and Exchange 2019. The EAC has the following options that you can work on and the rest has to be done on PowerShell:

- Recipients
- Permissions
- Compliance Management
- Organization

- Protection
- Mail flow
- Mobile
- Public Folders
- Unified Messaging
- Servers
- Hybrid

We won't be going through each tab and what it does as we covered this in an earlier chapter.

Viewing the commands that run in the background when the links in the EAC are clicked.

Everywhere you click and do things on the EAC has a PowerShell command running in the background. In Exchange 2010 this was on by default however in Exchange 2016 you first need to open the command logging window. To do this click the arrow next to the question mark (?) in the top right-hand corner and select **Show Command Logging.**

Figure 10.4 shows the steps:

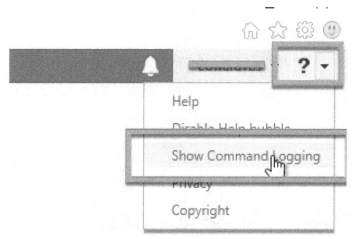

Figure 10.4*: Show command logging window.*

The command logging windows will open, see below *Figure 10.5:*

Figure 10.5: *Logging Viewer*

Now if you click on **Groups** you will see the command run as shown in *Figure 10.6* below:

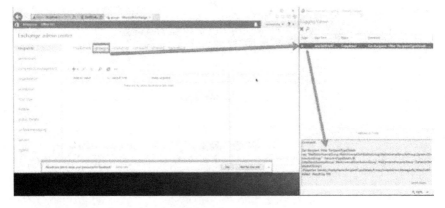

Figure 10.6: *Navigation in the EAC showing the command run in the background.*

That is how simple it is. If you close the Logging Viewer window and open it again, all the history will be gone, just be aware of that.

Conclusion

By now you should be familiar with how to work with the Exchange Admin Center as well as the Exchange Management Shell. You now know how to view the commands that are run in the Exchange Admin Center and how you can perform everything in the Exchange Management Shell for the more advanced IT Admin. You also know how to configure WinRM so that you can make use of remote PowerShell calls. As all the options in the Exchange Admin Center were explained in the earlier chapters, we briefly provided you a high overview of the EAC and also how you can limit access to the Exchange Admin Center due to the surface attack on the internet where they target Exchange servers.

In the next chapter and the final one of the book, you will have a good understanding of how to troubleshoot and solve some of the common issues that an Admin can encounter in there Exchange environment or there customers' environment.

Questions

1. **I can configure WinRM using the following options: Select 2.**

   a. Winrm qc

   b. Winrm quickconfig

   c. Winrm set

   Answer: a and b

2. **The cmdlets in Exchange 2010 can be used in Exchange 2016? (True or False)**

   Answer: True but Microsoft does advise you to use the newer ones.

3. **Exchange 2016 logging viewer is the same as Exchange 2010?**

   Answer: Incorrect, Exchange 2010 automatically shows you the commands run whereas Exchange 2016 you first have to open the Logging Viewer.

4. **Where can you manage public folders?**

   Answer: From the Exchange Admin center and with PowerShell.

5. **Are you able to configure everything in the Exchange Admin Center?**

   Answer: No, you need to use PowerShell to manage things not shown in the EAC.

CHAPTER 11

Troubleshooting Common Issues

Errors or problems in Exchange 2016 is something an admin does not look forward to. There are some errors that you cannot find help with on the internet and many people have blogs where they write about issues encountered but every environment is unique so some errors present themselves whereas others don't. In this chapter, you will learn how to troubleshoot some of the common errors or problems encountered in an environment. While this is not the full list of errors you will have an understanding of each one and where it applies.

Structure

Below is the list of items we can are common in an Exchange environment but not limited to:

- WinRM errors when launching the **Exchange Management Shell (EMS)**
- Full Exchange Installation disks due to all the logging.
- Error 400 when launching the Exchange Admin Center.
- Exchange Server freezing due to backups (Often posted on the forums)

- URL's not configured
- Certificate popups in Outlook.
- Cannot receive external email.
- Missing/Corrupt Exchange Security Groups in Active Directory.
- Anti-Virus Exclusions not set and as a result, it is scanning the `.EDB` file
- Installing unsupported .NET Framework versions with Windows Updates.
- Installation failures and watermarks.

Objectives

- Learn about winrm errors in Exchange and how to fix them.
- Learn about logging in Exchange 2016 and how it affects space.
- Learn about the client's connectivity and issues due to misconfigurations in Exchange.
- Learn about Anti-Virus and how it affects your applications.
- Learn about .NET and how an unsupported version can cause your exchange server to crash.

Let's briefly go through each one of these and explain them.

WinRM errors when launching the Exchange Management Shell (EMS)

In *Chapter 10: Exchange Management Shell vs. EAC,* we covered configuring WinRM but sometimes strict group policy and Anti-Virus can cause a block on WinRM and you need to allow it for your Exchange servers to run remote commands. If you have not configured WinRM then you need to do this as step1 and troubleshoot further after that.

Full Exchange Installation disks due to all the logging

Exchange 2013/2016 and Exchange 2019 all write a whole lot of logging data. This can fill up a 300 GB drive in 1 day if not monitored closely and correctly. This can also happen if Admins don't build servers properly in a sense that they give the Exchange Server minimum disk space and expect it to not grow. Exchange 2010 did not grow as quickly as the newer versions.

In my blog post below, I cover a lot of the logging information and have a script you can schedule to clear space on a daily or weekly basis. The most I have recovered is around 100 GB, others like 40-50 GB at a time. For more info on the logging and how to clear it out, you can go to the post here:

https://www.collaborationpro.com/exchange-2013-logging/

On a final note, please ensure that you use the Exchange 2016 calculator to build your server properly so you don't run into space issues.

Error 400 when launching the Exchange Admin Center

This error can be a result of a handful of things:

- Your authentication methods for OWA and ECP don't match.
- You have redirection enabled on the Default Website in IIS.
- Can be your bindings in IIS.

Not everyone will have the same symptom. Like we have mentioned in other sections, 3rd party applications can create problems by adding unnecessary bindings or enable redirection.

Exchange Server freezing due to backups (Often posted on the forums)

This problem where Exchange 2016 freezes is a common one. Some companies have backups run during the day or snapshot Exchange which causes a lockup of the server and disconnects all users. While snapshots are not supported, you need to move your backups to later in the evening or reach out to the vendor about the freezing.

URL's not configured

Sometimes it happens where Admins don't update the URLs on Exchange and do not understand why it won't just work. For exchange 2016 or any version, as a matter of fact, you need to configure your URLs to match your SSL certificate. Other times company A merges with Company B and the URLS is not updated.

As part of your installation and configuration you need to configure this, it is one of the important pieces in Exchange. This is where clients will connect to for ActiveSync, **Outlook on the Web (OWA)**, etc.

Certificate popups in Outlook

This is quite a broad problem in Exchange/Outlook. While some forget to configure URLs to match the SSL certificate or do not configure a certificate for external use but have configured the URLs this will cause popups. Other instances where this happens is when Firewalls/Load balancers are not updated with the new SSL certificate and this will cause popups on Outlook.

If AD Permissions are incorrectly applied for the OAB then this will also cause popup issues. Third-party vendors that work on top of Exchange can also cause this.

Cannot receive external email

One of the biggest issues is when Admins install an Exchange 2016 Server and things don't work as expected like they cannot receive any external mail. If the receive connector has not been configured to allow anonymous email, it will bounce or if you have no MX records in place email will never reach your site.

You need to ensure that you have your receive connectors configured and that your ISP knows of your new Exchange 2016 server so they can add it to the list of IP's to route mail.

Missing/Corrupt Exchange Security Groups in Active Directory

This issue seems to be happening more often where Admins either remove the groups or they get corrupted. These groups are vital as it is how you control RBAC of who has access to do what. It is easy to reinstate this by simply running the following command:

```
Setup /IAcceptExchangeServerLicenseTerms /PrepareAD
```

Do not leave the groups broken or missing.

Anti-Virus Exclusions not set and as a result, it is scanning the .EDB file

With each version of Exchange Microsoft highlight what needs to be excluded in Anti-Virus products to avoid problems where AV deletes log files or scans the `.EDB` files. If you have ESET, Webroot, Symantec, etc. installed, go to documents website for Microsoft and ensure that all file and folder exclusions are set.

Installing unsupported .NET Framework versions with Windows Updates

Exchange 2016 Cumulative Updates work with certain versions of .NET Framework. Microsoft has a support matrix on which they list the supported versions. On the Exchange blogs, they also announce support or no support for a version of .NET Framework. For example, .NET Framework 4.7 is not supported on any version.

The challenge comes in if the Admin does not let the SCCM or WSUS admin know and they release this version for installation. This can break Exchange and will result in performing a recovery.

Installation failures and watermarks

Most installations of Exchange 2016 or upgrades go through without an error but sometimes an upgrade or install fails and this leaves keys in the registry called watermarks and Admins don't remove this and re-attempt to run the installation or upgrade and it keeps failing because of this. It is not just 1 key that can have the issue so it will be difficult to list but if you navigate to HKLM\Sofware\Microsoft\ ExchangeServer\V15\XXXXX

XXXXX will be where you need to go to remove the key. Re-run the upgrade or setup and it should succeed.

Conclusion

You now have reached the end of the book. You have learnt how to deal with common problems and how to remediate them. You should now have a sense of what you can experience in a customer environment or your environment. Overall you now have a better understanding of what Exchange 2016 is and how to install and configure it in your environment and as well as customer environments you will be managing.